I0418762

Politely Rejecting Jesus

Dan Kapr

Enersin Press

ISBN: 979-8-9853324-4-5 (paperback)
ISBN: 979-8-9853324-5-2 (ebook)

Enersin Press
919 W 34th St #4713
Baltimore, MD 21211

dankapr.com

For Kristen

Table of contents

Preface

This is a book about Jesus and why I stopped worshiping him. It's a book that I wish I'd been able to read when I was a teenager, since it could have saved me a considerable amount of confusion and heartbreak. My hope is that it will help other people who are struggling with the same sorts of questions that I puzzled over for many years before finally realizing that my faith in Jesus was ill-placed. Or maybe, if nothing else, it will help explain why the arguments found in popular Christian books like *The Case for Christ* are not all they're cracked up to be.[1]

Why do this "politely"? I am inclined to think that arguments against widely cherished religious beliefs work better when you're not attacking the people who hold them. When I was younger, I sincerely believed that there were strong arguments in favor of Christianity. Hearing my beliefs mocked and misrepresented by certain writers only motivated me to dig my feet in further. As a result, I was more resistant to correction than I needed to be. I don't want to create the same obstacle for anyone else. Furthermore, since I am still a theist, I think it's important to show that rejecting the Christian view of Jesus need not involve a rejection of everything that he talked about, and somehow I don't think that making fun of Christians is the best way to get this message across.

Although I have a background in ministry and a master's degree from New Brunswick Theological Seminary, I am not a scholar. However, at different points it is important to know what most New Testament scholars think about this or that issue. To make sure I was not speaking out of ignorance, I consulted a number of resources that are used in intro-level New Testament courses in universities and seminaries across the country. These resources are produced by scholars for the purpose of acquainting the reader with standard views in the field. I've listed them in a short bibliography at the end of the book for anyone who is interested.

I am immensely grateful for all of the encouragement and support I received from my friends as I worked on this project. I want to express my warmest thanks to everyone who gave me any kind of help or feedback, including Andie Basto, Steve Boyland, Abby Fanara, Ryan Lina, Alexa Sciuto, Cami Sotela, and Barry Wright. And I owe a huge debt of love and gratitude to Kristen McKenzie, not only for reading the book and offering a ton of helpful input about how to make it better, but also for being an incredible partner and an all-around amazing person (not to mention a ridiculously talented performer and improv teacher). I feel so lucky to have ended up with the life that I have.

Glossary

apologetics The defense of Christian beliefs based on an appeal to arguments and evidence.

ascension The moment when Jesus was taken up to heaven.

doctrine An official Christian teaching.

final judgment The event at the end of history when God will reward the righteous and punish the wicked.

Galilee The northern region of Israel (in first-century Palestine) where the town of Nazareth was located.

heresy A theological teaching that undermines essential Christian doctrines.

imminent Happening in the very near future.

Judea The southern region of Israel (in first-century Palestine) where the cities of Bethlehem and Jerusalem were located.

Messiah A deliverer who, in Jesus' time, was expected to liberate the Jewish people and establish God's kingdom.

New Testament The second half of the Christian Bible containing Christian literature written after the death of Jesus.

Old Testament The first half of the Christian Bible containing Jewish literature written long before the birth of Jesus.

Q A hypothetical source that is widely thought to have been used by the authors who wrote the gospels of Matthew and Luke.

resurrection The raising of a dead person back to life, or the raising of all people back to life at the end of history.

second coming The future return of Jesus to earth.

Son of Man A heavenly figure who, in Jesus' time, was expected to appear at the end of history and enact God's final judgment.

theology A system of beliefs about God.

Chapter 1
The Son of God

I parted ways with the Christian community over a decade ago, and since then I have learned to be suspicious of religious institutions. However, I am not an anti-religious person. If there is a divine reality out there, it seems sensible for people to seek a deeper connection with it. And this book is not meant to discourage anyone from doing that, especially since I continue to embrace theism myself. Nor do I want to discourage people from paying attention to what Jesus says. Some of his words still resonate deeply with me, even after all these years of being outside the church.

Don't get me wrong. My experience with Christianity was not all sunshine and rainbows. I grew up in a fundamentalist setting where a number of disturbing ideas were hammered into my head—for instance, that I was evil from birth, that I deserved to be tormented for all eternity, and that, on many occasions in the past, God had called for (if not carried out himself) the brutal execution of numerous people, including children and infants (see 1 Samuel 15:1–3).

To be fair, I was also told that God loved me, but it's hard to take comfort in this when you think that God would be willing to toss you into a lake of fire just because of the way you were born. The fact that Jesus once made a comment about an "unforgivable sin" (which he described as blasphemy of the Holy Spirit without going into great detail about what that means) certainly didn't help. It's enough to give a person several anxiety disorders.

And yet, in spite of all this, there is still something very moving about Jesus' vision of God. It's not when he talks about hellfire and unforgivable sins. Rather, it's when he tells his disciples about a man who left ninety-nine sheep behind just to find the one that got lost. Obviously, one sheep won't make a huge difference, economically speaking, to a man who already has ninety-nine others. A shepherd who leaves the flock to pursue a single sheep might seem reckless. But Jesus describes the man as rejoicing jubilantly when he finds the missing sheep, and he says that this is what God is like with us (Matthew 18:12–14).

Better still is Jesus' story about the final judgment, a scenario that evangelical preachers have frequently used to scare people into converting to Christianity. What makes it so strange is that *their* version of the final judgment does not seem to match the version that Jesus talked about. In the typical evangelical version, the human sinner stands before God, convicted of their sins. If, at some point during their time on earth, they asked for God's forgiveness and placed their faith in Jesus, then they are rewarded with eternal life. If not, they are exiled to hell forever.

However, in Jesus' version of the final judgment, the people who are deemed worthy of eternal life are the ones who visited him when he was sick or in prison, who clothed him when he was naked, and who fed him when he was hungry. When the people on trial are understandably confused by this (since they don't remember ever feeding or clothing their divine judge), he explains that anytime they did it for anyone else, they were doing it for him (see Matthew 25:31–46).

This theological framework insists that a person's value does not come from their wealth, social status, or religious identity. Even prophets who perform miracles—even those who do it *in Jesus' name*—are not automatically given a pass. Jesus says elsewhere that they are completely missing the point if they think that their acts of power make any spiritual difference (see Matthew 7:21–23). What really matters is how they treated other people.

What makes this framework so compelling is the thought that, in taking care of each other, we are participating in something sacred. Jesus speaks of a God who identifies with people who are lonely and hurting. This is why special provisions are made for those who struggle with poverty, grief, and illness, and for anyone else whom society deems untouchable or unlovable. Taken seriously, this is a blueprint for a kingdom (or a country or community or whatever you want to call it) where nobody gets the upper hand over anyone else, and nobody needs to make a name for themselves. Right or wrong, this vision of God is powerful.

Unfortunately, its power is obscured by how badly represented it is in our culture. There's nothing more joyless than hearing these ideas filtered through bland sermons, hateful political speeches, and passive aggressive comments from family members. Nevertheless, in your lowest moments, when you have no hope left and when nobody else seems to realize how much you're hurting, to actually *believe* that there is a power behind the universe that embraces you, identifies with you, and feels affection toward you, can be indescribably comforting. While Jesus isn't the only one who ever spoke of a God like this, he seems to have had a knack for getting that message across.

Losing My Faith

At an earlier point in my life, I found Jesus' vision of a kind and merciful God to be intoxicating. Christian apologetics resources (which are focused on presenting arguments and evidence for the rationality of Christian beliefs) convinced me that my faith in Jesus was well-placed, so I set out to pursue a life in ministry. After college, I spent a few

years working as a youth pastor, and then I entered a seminary with
the intention of becoming either a senior pastor, a Bible professor, or
both. But during my time at seminary, my life took an unexpected turn.
Christianity stopped making sense to me, and I realized that most of
what I'd learned in church was wrong. By the time I graduated with my
ministry degree, I was no longer a Christian.

So, why did I stop worshiping Jesus? For one thing, I'm not sure if
he actually wanted anyone to put him on the same level as God. Maybe
he did, but that seems like something we'd want to be quite sure about
before falling down at his feet and devoting our lives to him. More
importantly, regardless of what Jesus may have claimed about himself,
there are good reasons not to treat him like a deity. I say this because of
some extremely problematic issues that come up in his teachings, which
we will begin to explore in the next chapter. In other words, as much as
I love certain parts of Jesus' message, there are other parts that can't be
ignored and, in my opinion, should not be embraced.

Some people might ask, "So what if Jesus is not really God? If his
vision of God is as compelling as you've made it out to be, why not
embrace the symbolism? Why not align yourself with that vision of the
kingdom where the poor are blessed and the meek inherit the earth? Why
break away from the community that Jesus started?"

Believe me, if I could have made it work, I would have. I was very
familiar with more liberal Christian approaches to Jesus, which place less
emphasis on the historical integrity of the gospels and more emphasis
on the way that Jesus reveals the heart and character of God. I would
have stayed in the church for the rest of my life if I could have reconciled
my conscience with this kind of Christianity. Unfortunately, it faces
its own major problems, which I'll be touching on at different points
throughout our discussion.

My goal in this book, then, is to explain why I stopped worshiping Jesus, and in the rest of this chapter I will set the stage for how I will be approaching this topic. Before we begin, however, I want to state for the record that, in my opinion, the fact that certain parts of Jesus' message resonate so deeply with so many people (including myself) is a sign that he was hitting on something real.

Personally, I've come to think that one can continue to embrace those compelling images for God—the shepherd who seeks the lost sheep, the judge who identifies with the oppressed—with full intellectual integrity, even after rejecting the framework in which Jesus presents these ideas. It looks and feels a bit different outside of that framework, of course, and theism of any kind requires its own justification (and so will remain a matter of debate among intelligent minds), but one can certainly do worse than to believe in a God who promotes empathy and compassion.

Jesus and the Christian God

The central claim of the Christian faith is that Jesus Christ died for our sins, rose from the dead, and will someday return to earth. In the earliest centuries of the church's history, Christian theologians realized that their faith in Jesus required a belief in his divinity. If Jesus was an ordinary human, then he was no less in need of redemption than the rest of us. In that case, his death would not be able to provide atonement for our sins. Thus, the basic Christian story about Jesus did not seem to work without an emphasis on his divinity. If you deny that Jesus is God, you undermine the claim that he died for our sins and secured our salvation.

Affirming the divinity of Jesus sounds simple enough, but Christianity began as a Jewish movement, and one of the features it inherited from Judaism was a deep commitment to monotheism, the idea that there is only one God. But how can there only be one God if Jesus is divine? The gospels in the New Testament portray Jesus as praying to God. Does this mean that Jesus was praying to himself? Furthermore, the New Testament frequently refers to Jesus as the Son of God. Does this mean that Jesus is his own Son?

The Christian response to all of this is to invoke the doctrine of the Trinity. Even though Christians believe in one God, they also believe that there are three different persons called God—God the Father, God the Son, and God the Holy Spirit. In that case, what does it mean to say that there is only one God? Christian theology answers that there is only a single divine substance, or in other words, a single entity possessing a divine nature. *One substance, three persons.* This doctrine provides a framework in which Christians can try to make sense out of the relationship between Jesus and God.

Whether it's a profound truth or an outrageous absurdity, the doctrine of the Trinity lies at the foundation of all Christian thinking about Jesus. Ever since the fourth century C.E., mainstream Christianity has been firmly committed to both the unity of God and the distinct identities of the three divine persons. For Christians, there are not three gods, nor is God a single person. On the traditional view, both of these alternatives are heresies.

Now, when Christians say that God became a human being, they don't mean "God" in the full trinitarian sense, since it was not the Father or the Holy Spirit who became human. Rather, it was the second person of the Trinity who entered into human life and lived among us about two thousand years ago. This is the doctrine of the incarnation. The word *incarnation* comes from a Latin term which means "to be made flesh." For Christians, Jesus is the real human embodiment of God.

Most Christians throughout history have treated the incarnation as a literal, historical fact, but a good number of modern Christians have moved away from this kind of thinking. Instead, they regard the incarnation as a metaphor. They see Jesus as revealing the character of God in a definitive way, without possessing the literal mind of God. Some theologians go further and say that all language about God is metaphorical. On their view, it's a mistake to worry about the logical coherence of a concept like the Trinity, because the idea is not meant to be taken literally.

Of course, Christians who take the incarnation metaphorically still sing to Jesus in church as if he is the creator of the universe, and this may seem a little disjointed. Personally, I'm not convinced that a metaphorical treatment of Christianity's core doctrines makes sense. Part of the reason is that if all language about God is metaphorical, then to say that "God exists" is to speak metaphorically. In that case, God does not exist in any literal sense, and no metaphorical description of God can actually be true, since there is no reality to which any such description applies. In other words, this approach to theology is self-defeating. If the response is to pretend that Christian theology is compatible with an atheistic view of reality, then we are no longer really dealing with Christianity at all.

I'll have a little more to say about metaphorical approaches to Christian theology when I talk about the resurrection of Jesus. For now, we'll keep our focus on the traditional approach.

So what do Christians mean when they call Jesus the Son of God? In one sense, they mean that Jesus is God's literal offspring. Christians say that Jesus was "begotten" by God, and this is usually taken as a reference to his birth. According to the New Testament, Jesus' mother conceived him before she'd ever had sex. She was impregnated by God (not through sexual intercourse but simply by God's power), and thus Jesus had no human father.

Being the Son of God can also have symbolic meaning. For instance, one of the psalms in the Old Testament has God referring to the king of Israel as his son. The psalmist, speaking from the perspective of the king, writes, "I will tell of the decree of the Lord: He said to me, 'You are my son; today I have begotten you'" (Psalm 2:7).

This psalm was probably recited as part of the king's coronation ceremony, meaning that the king was thought to become the Son of God on the day he began to rule over the kingdom. Although the psalm uses the language of "begetting," it does not mean that the king is the literal offspring of God. Rather, it means that he has a special relationship with God, and that he is God's chosen representative on earth. The New Testament applies this verse to Jesus in a couple of places.

Finally, Christians call Jesus the Son of God because, on their view, the second member of the Trinity relates to the first the way that a son relates to a father. This raises the question of whether the Trinity implies some sort of hierarchy within God. After all, why should the Son submit to the Father if they are equal in power, wisdom, and authority? Christians do not all agree on this topic, but most seem to affirm that Jesus was already the Son of God *before* he became a human.

The Humanity of Jesus

If you're a nonbeliever, you might think that it would be pretty easy to refute the Christian view of Jesus. After all, if Jesus is God, and God knows everything, then Jesus must know everything too, right? In that case, if Jesus ever said anything false, then he couldn't have been God. All we need to do, then, is figure out if Jesus ever made any false statements.

But the problem with this simple logic is that Christianity has always affirmed the full humanity of Jesus.

This point is crucial for understanding everything that follows, so it deserves careful attention. Christians do not believe that Jesus was a half-divine, half-human hybrid, nor do they believe that a divine person simply wore a human body the way that an actor wears a costume. Jesus' humanity was not an illusion. Rather, in addition to having all the essential attributes of divinity (whatever those are), Jesus also had all the essential attributes of humanity. He was truly God and truly human.

If Jesus was truly human, then he must have had a real human mind and consciousness. This creates important problems for the bare assertion that "Jesus knew everything," since being a real person composed of flesh and blood seems to imply certain limitations in his knowledge. This view has firm biblical support, since Jesus sometimes displays a lack of knowledge in the gospels, like when he faces a crowd of people and asks them, "Who touched my cloak?" (Mark 5:30).

Some people might tell you that, when Jesus was a baby, he could have easily explained the periodic table of elements in perfect English (even though his family's language was Aramaic). I'm not sure if any serious Christian theologian would endorse this view. If Jesus was really human, then his brain had to develop the same way other human brains do. His thoughts and his conception of the world around him depended on his physical and psychological development.

This might sound sacrilegious, but it's fully in line with mainstream Christian theology. After all, it is the heart of Christian faith to believe that Jesus died, and this would have been impossible if he had not been mortal. Otherwise, when the Romans crucified Jesus, he would have just hung up there on the cross until they let him down. If Jesus was really mortal, as Christians believe, then he could be made to bleed, feel pain, and lose consciousness. If you bashed him in the head with a blunt instrument, he could be made to suffer brain damage.

As a real human being, Jesus had to learn how to walk and speak when he was growing up, and the growing process must have involved a fair amount of trial and error. What do I mean by "error"? Imagine the baby Jesus with his parents, Mary and Joseph. They're trying to help him learn how to walk. If you deny Jesus' humanity, you might picture something out of a Superman comic: they stand the baby on his feet and let go, and then he takes off running all over the house at lightning speed, without ever getting tired. Would such a creature count as human? It seems doubtful. An authentically human baby Jesus would probably do the same thing that all babies do when placed on their feet for the first time—he would wobble and then fall on his butt. This is technically a failure, but it's also a necessary part of growth.

What about learning how to be a carpenter? Would Jesus have been a master craftsman from the moment he took up his father's trade? Again, if it were a Superman comic, one could imagine Jesus coming out of Joseph's workshop holding up an exquisite, Victorian-style rocking chair: "How did I do, father?" But as a real human being, Jesus' first attempt at carpentry probably wasn't very pretty to look at. None of us can become proficient in any skill without trying and failing, because we need to learn how to master the relevant techniques, and our minds must be trained to recognize good quality work. To say that Jesus emerged from his mother's womb fully capable of walking, speaking, crafting, and reasoning is to deny his full humanity, the very thing that Christianity says is non-negotiable.

Here I must point out that there is often a big divide between what Christianity teaches and what you might hear from any random person you encounter in a church setting. Some Christians who have not paid much attention to their own spiritual heritage will aggressively deny certain things about Jesus' humanity. *Of course he knew English! Of course he had a complete understanding of nuclear physics! Of course he didn't go to the bathroom!* And so on. Their Jesus is not a human Jesus, and in that sense, they are heretics of their own religion. But it's highly doubtful that the church they attend would officially endorse their views. Since the first century, Christian communities have, with few exceptions, strongly affirmed the humanity of Jesus.

The New Testament says that Jesus became like us in every way, except that he never sinned (Hebrews 2:17; 4:15). Why does this matter? Because as far as I can tell, there's no sin involved in making mistakes as one learns how to walk, speak, or build a table. I'd even venture to say that there's no sin involved in accidentally getting the details of a story wrong, or in not knowing about scientific facts that haven't been discovered yet. If the doctrine of the incarnation is correct, and if Jesus had a real human mind and brain, this seems to give Christians some leeway when talking about the extent of his knowledge.

For instance, at one point in the gospels, Jesus attributes one of the psalms to King David (see Mark 12:36), even though scholars doubt that David actually wrote it. Does this prove that he's not God? Back when I was a Christian, I would have said no. In fact, I would have said that it's a boring detail to get hung up on. Again, in the Gospel of Mark, Jesus gets the name of a high priest wrong when referring to a story from the Old Testament (Mark 2:26).[1] Christian apologists have sometimes gone to ridiculous lengths to explain away this error, but it seems like a simple mistake that anyone could have made.

I've been emphasizing the humanity of Jesus because it's important to make sure we're not holding Christianity to a standard that it doesn't claim to meet. Nevertheless, there must be a limit on how much error or failure we can attribute to Jesus without calling his divinity into question. It would obviously be a mistake to worship Jesus if, say, he declared that there was a tiny man living in his finger, or if he told his followers that the key to everlasting life is to drink a gallon of water infused with hemlock.

So where is the line between an error that can be reconciled with Jesus' divinity and an error that can't? Perhaps a better way to approach this question would be to focus on issues that affect Jesus' *spiritual authority* rather than his knowledge. Spiritual authority, in this context, would mean that someone is a credible spokesperson for God. Thus, if Jesus really is God, then he speaks with spiritual authority. To deny this, I think, would lead to a denial of Christianity. On the other hand, if Jesus' spiritual authority is compromised by his teachings, then we would seem to be justified in rejecting his divinity.

Chapter 2

False Prophecies

Christianity teaches that Jesus ascended to heaven and will someday return to earth. For many Christians, this will involve an event called "the rapture." This is supposed to be the moment when all the Christians in the world will suddenly vanish, leaving everything behind including their clothes. In the blink of an eye, Christians will find themselves up in the clouds with Jesus, and then they'll return with him to heaven, wearing nothing but a smile. Those who are left behind on earth will face a time of great suffering called the tribulation, brought about by the reign of the Antichrist.

When I was little, everyone I knew seemed to think that the rapture would happen at any moment. I remember seeing glass-encased VHS tapes hanging on the walls of people's homes, emblazoned with the words, "In case of rapture break glass." These tapes contained information for those who would be left behind, to teach them about Jesus and prepare them for what lay ahead. I sometimes wonder if these strange artifacts still exist. Were they ever transferred to digital media?

In any case, our belief in the rapture's imminence, or nearness, was grounded in our understanding of the Bible. In the Gospel of Matthew, Jesus' disciples ask him, "What will be the sign of your coming and of the end of the age?" Jesus, in a classic teacher move, answers with a whole discourse. He explains that, toward the end, there will be certain catastrophic events in the world, including wars, famines, and earthquakes. His followers will be tortured and killed for their devotion to him, and false prophets will lead many people astray. These events will immediately precede Jesus' appearance (see Matthew 24:3–31).

Leaving the Rapture Behind

In college, I learned that most Christians don't believe in the rapture. I found this bewildering at first, because my beliefs were heavily influenced by a form of Christian theology called *dispensationalism*. Its name comes from the fact that it treats history as a series of "dispensations," or different ages in which God relates to his people in different ways.

Most dispensationalists split the second coming of Jesus into two events: the rapture and the glorious appearing. The rapture is supposed to be a secret return, meaning that Jesus will come back to earth, but only very briefly, and without being seen by any non-Christians. Then, after the tribulation, he is supposed to appear on earth again, visibly and in all his glory, to set up his kingdom and conquer the Devil.

In spite of how popular this kind of theology has become, it only dates back to the nineteenth century. The majority of Christians either reject dispensationalism or are part of a tradition that was never touched by it. They typically treat the second coming of Jesus as a singular event, and they do so for good reason. When the New Testament speaks about the future return of Jesus, it doesn't make a distinction between the rapture and the glorious appearing.

Soon and Very Soon

While widespread belief in the rapture is a modern development, the idea that Jesus is coming back soon is certainly not. Dispensationalists did not invent it. Quite the contrary, it is written all over the New Testament:

Strengthen your hearts, for the coming of the Lord is near. (James 5:8)

The end of all things is near. (1 Peter 4:7)

In a very little while, the one who is coming will come and will not delay. (Hebrews 10:37)

Children, it is the last hour! As you have heard that antichrist is coming, so now many antichrists have come. From this we know that it is the last hour. (1 John 2:18)

The one who testifies to these things says, "Surely I am coming soon." Amen. Come, Lord Jesus! (Revelation 22:20)

The New Testament repeatedly affirms that the end is near, and that Jesus' return is just around the corner. This would seem to pose a major problem for Christianity, since it has been about two thousand years since these words were written, and Christians are still waiting for this promise to be fulfilled.

Or are they? Apparently some Christians believe that the second coming took place back in the first century, though I have never met anyone like this myself. But this approach is extremely uncommon and, if I understand it correctly, it does not hold that Jesus literally returned to earth and sat down upon a literal throne from which he has been reigning for the past two millennia. Instead it suggests that, after Jesus ascended to heaven, he manifested his power on earth through the destruction of

Jerusalem. The connection between Jesus' return and the destruction of Jerusalem is supplied by the "end times" discourse that I mentioned earlier. Since the Romans destroyed Jerusalem and the temple back in 70 C.E., some Christians think that this event fulfilled Jesus' predictions about the second coming.

The glaring problem with this approach (does it even need to be said?) is that the New Testament does not just say that Jesus is coming back soon; it also says that when he comes back, the dead will be raised and God's enemies will be defeated (1 Corinthians 15:23–26). The return of Jesus is supposed to put an end to the present age marked by sin and death. I take it as given, then, that Jesus has not come back, and thankfully the vast majority of Christians are sensible enough to agree.

A False Hope

Since Jesus hasn't returned, what are we supposed to make of the promise that he will return in the near future? In the second letter of Peter, the author acknowledges that some people will take the delay of Jesus' return as proof that the original promise was false. However, he encourages his readers to remember that with God, "one day is like a thousand years, and a thousand years are like one day." It may seem like God is taking a long time from our perspective, but from God's perspective, things are right on schedule. If Jesus hasn't returned yet, it's only because he is trying to give people as much time to repent of their sins as possible (2 Peter 3:3–9).

These ideas sound great until you stop to think about them. Consider the claim that Jesus' return is not actually delayed if you look at it from God's perspective. If Jesus is only coming back "soon" from God's point of view, then we have no way of knowing what comments like "the end is near" and "the coming of the Lord is near" are supposed to mean, since God's point of view eludes us. But this only seems to undermine the spiritual value of the New Testament. What good is a promise that nobody can understand?

This is an important point so I don't want to rush past it. In ordinary conversation, it's usually easy to figure out what people mean when they speak of imminent returns. It all depends on the context. For example, if your spouse texts "See you soon" while leaving work, and it takes an hour for them to get home, it would be silly for you to feel disappointed if they didn't walk through the door in the next few minutes. And if your boss tells you that you'll soon be promoted, you may not know exactly what "soon" means, but if two years go by and you're still in the same position, you'd be justified in concluding that your boss lied to you.

Now imagine your boss saying, "Great news! You'll be promoted soon, but it's only 'soon' from a management perspective, and I may postpone it if it will help the company, even for decades if I have to." A promise like that is hardly something to get excited about. So if the promise that "Jesus is coming back soon" really means that Jesus is not coming back for thousands of years, it completely undermines the rationale for suggesting that he's coming back soon in the first place. One might as well just say, "Jesus will be back again someday," and leave it at that. But that's not what the New Testament does.

Some Christians interpret the biblical promises about the second coming as meaning that Jesus will return suddenly, at any moment, but not necessarily soon. Of course, this only solves the problem by refusing to look at it. The New Testament says quite clearly that "it is the last hour," "the end of all things is near," and Jesus is coming "in a very little while." And here we are, two thousand years later, still waiting. It turns out that, back in the first century, the end was nowhere in sight.

Could the delay of the second coming be an act of divine mercy? Is God just giving people more time to repent of their sin? The problem here is that the ongoing march of history only seems to greatly increase the number of people who will die without believing in Jesus as Lord. If salvation depends on faith in Jesus, then the longer Jesus takes to return, the more people God will have to condemn, unless God is going to save everyone, in which case it's false to say that we need more time to repent anyway. More importantly, *the number of people that God is trying to save is irrelevant,* because the original promise was that Jesus would return soon, not that he would return soon unless he needed to save more people. There is just no way to avoid the fact that, over and over again, the New Testament affirms a false hope.

Paul and the Second Coming

Traditionally, the New Testament was thought to have been written by people who knew Jesus directly or who witnessed his resurrection. Many of the books are attributed either to Jesus' disciples or his brothers. If these attributions are correct, then some of the people who knew Jesus personally—including Peter, John, and James—are on record as teaching that he will return quickly.

However, many traditional views of authorship have been challenged by New Testament scholars in the past few centuries. Scholars often deny that Peter, John, or James wrote any letters at all, in light of their lower-class status and the fact that literacy rates were quite low at the time. The books bearing their names are often treated as pseudonymous literature. In other words, the letter of James wasn't written by James, but by someone else who was (for reasons unknown to us) writing in James' name. As for the book of Revelation, it really was written by a man named John, so it is not pseudonymous, but the author is not usually thought to be the same person as Jesus' disciple John.

These modern scholarly views of the New Testament seem to offer a way for the Christian to get around the problem of Jesus' delayed return, since they raise the possibility that Jesus' original followers never actually taught that he would return soon. Couldn't it just be a mistaken religious belief that only came about later? To answer this question, we have to look at the evidence and think like detectives. (Actually, we have to think like historians, but it's more fun to call ourselves detectives.)

The earliest surviving Christian documents are the authentic letters of Paul, which were written mostly (if not entirely) during the 50s of the first century C.E. Of the thirteen letters attributed to Paul in the New Testament, seven are universally accepted as authentic.[1] Although Paul was not one of Jesus' original followers, he was personally acquainted with Peter, James, and other Christian leaders, and he often makes use of early Christian oral traditions. Thus, even if we don't possess any writings from anyone who knew Jesus personally, Paul provides us with valuable insight about what the Christian movement was like in its earliest stages.

In one letter, Paul explains why Christians shouldn't be bothered by the fact that some of their fellow believers have already died. He tells his readers not to grieve like those who have no hope, and he says that when Jesus returns, those who died will be resurrected (1 Thessalonians 4:13–18). It's worth asking why Paul wrote these words, since future generations of Christians would presumably already believe that God had a plan for Christians who died. If Christians knew that they might be waiting a long time for Jesus to come back, the fact that some of them had already died would hardly seem remarkable or confusing. Since Paul found it necessary to comfort at least one grieving Christian community by explaining that those who died will still be saved, they must have been expecting Jesus to return within their lifetimes.

Not only that, but we can be quite sure that Paul shared this expectation. In the same passage, he seems to assume that he'll be among those who are still alive when Jesus returns: "Then we who are alive, who are left, will be caught up in the clouds together with them to meet the Lord in the air" (1 Thessalonians 4:17). In another letter, Paul plainly states that he and his contemporaries are those "on whom the ends of the ages have come" (1 Corinthians 10:11). Elsewhere he claims that salvation is close, the night is far gone, and the day is just about to arrive (Romans 13:11–12). There is no doubt that Paul expected Jesus to return in the very near future.

The Resurrection of the Messiah

Is it possible to know what other Christian leaders besides Paul would have said about this? Let's dig a bit further. At the end of one letter, Paul uses an Aramaic phrase, "Marana tha," which means, "Our Lord, come" (1 Corinthians 16:22). This might seem strange, since Paul's letters are all written in Greek, as is the rest of the New Testament. Why would Paul suddenly use an Aramaic phrase here? The key is to remember that Aramaic was the primary (if not only) language of Jesus and his disciples. In all likelihood, Paul is reciting a prayer that originated in the days when most Christians spoke Aramaic. It seems that Christians have been waiting for Jesus to return since the earliest days of their movement.

Now, in the same letter where he recites the Aramaic prayer, Paul also preserves an early creedal formula which says that Christ died for our sins, rose from the dead, and was seen alive by various witnesses. Paul makes it clear that this is the same message the other apostles were preaching: "Whether then it was I or they, so we proclaim and so you believed" (1 Corinthians 15:3–11).

This is an important piece of information. Two of the witnesses mentioned in the creed are Jesus' disciple Peter (called by his Aramaic name Cephas) and James, who was one of Jesus' brothers. In a different letter, Paul airs a bit of dirty laundry concerning a dispute he had with both of these men (Galatians 2:11–14). Since Paul could be quite candid about their disagreements, his testimony about their points of agreement is likely to be reliable. Between this and the fact that the creedal formula is an early tradition, we have strong grounds for concluding that Jesus' original followers proclaimed him as the resurrected Christ.

Here's why this matters. In the Old Testament, the resurrection was an event that was supposed to happen after a time of great suffering. This comes up in the book of Daniel, which was written to address the fact that God's faithful people were being brutally persecuted by their non-Jewish rulers. Even though they were experiencing terrible suffering, a time was coming when they would be rescued not just from their political enemies, but from death itself. In one passage, the author says that God will raise his righteous people back to life and reward them with glorious immortality (Daniel 12:1–3).

Many people at the time of Jesus expected that God's final victory over evil would be enacted by some kind of redeemer or deliverer, but they had different ideas about what this meant. In the passage from Daniel that we just discussed, God's people are rescued by the angel Michael. But there is another passage in Daniel that speaks of the coming of "one like a son of man," who is given authority over all the kingdoms of the earth (Daniel 7:13–14). In its original context, the phrase "son of man" means "human being," so the figure in this prophecy is meant to be understood as someone who looks like a human.

Because of this passage in Daniel, some Jewish writings from around the time of Jesus express a belief that God will eventually send a cosmic judge called the Son of Man. Other writings anticipate a human figure called the Messiah. Many Jewish people expected the Messiah to be a descendant of David, the famous king from the Old Testament. They were waiting for this figure to free the people of Israel and permanently restore their political independence.

This sheds important light on what the early Christians meant when they proclaimed Jesus as the resurrected Christ (a term which literally means "Messiah"). The resurrection and the Messiah were both "end times" concepts. Granted, we are not necessarily talking about the end of the space-time universe. In this context, phrases like "the end of the world" and "the last days" may simply refer to the end of the present age marked by death and suffering. Of course, some passages do speak about the destruction of the physical world (such as 2 Peter 3:10–13), but the destruction is followed by a new creation. In any case, to say that the Messiah had come and that he had been raised from the dead was to declare that we were now living in the last days.

This is why Paul connects Jesus' resurrection to the general resurrection and to the hope that Jesus would soon defeat God's enemies (1 Corinthians 15:12–28). In Paul's cultural context, to proclaim Jesus as the resurrected Messiah without suggesting that the end was quickly approaching would have seemed confusing, if not completely incoherent. Thus, if the proclamation of Jesus as the resurrected Messiah goes back to the very beginning of the Christian movement—and it certainly does—so must the expectation for him to return quickly.

In short, we cannot escape the fact that the early Christians expected Jesus to return in the near future, probably within their lifetimes. The real question for us is whether this expectation has anything to do with the message that Jesus preached.

Was Jesus Misunderstood?

At the end of the Gospel of John, we find an interesting conversation between Peter and the newly resurrected Jesus. After Jesus makes a cryptic prediction about how Peter will eventually die, their attention turns to one of the other disciples:

> When Peter saw him, he said to Jesus, "Lord, what about him?" Jesus said to him, "If it is my will that he remain until I come, what is that to you? Follow me!" So the rumor spread among the brothers and sisters that this disciple would not die. Yet Jesus did not say to him that he would not die, but, "If it is my will that he remain until I come, what is that to you?" (John 21:20–23)

Apparently there was a rumor going around in the Christian world that this one particular disciple would not die before Jesus returned, and the rumor was allegedly based on something Jesus said. But the author of this gospel is adamant that Jesus' words were misunderstood.

Earlier I mentioned that, in Jesus' time, some people were looking forward to the arrival of a heavenly figure called the Son of Man, based on their interpretation of a prophecy from Daniel. In the gospels, Jesus identifies himself with this figure, though he often speaks about himself in the third person. This is where Christianity runs into a monumental difficulty, because even though John denies that Jesus promised a quick return, the first three gospels tell a different story. The Gospel of Mark records Jesus as saying the following:

> "Those who are ashamed of me and of my words in this adulterous and sinful generation, of them the Son of Man will also be ashamed when he comes in the glory of his Father with the holy angels." And he said to them, "Truly I tell you, there are some standing here who will not taste death until they see that the kingdom of God has come with power." (Mark 8:38–9:1)

> "Then they will see 'the Son of Man coming in clouds' with great power and glory. Then he will send out the angels and gather the elect from the four winds, from the ends of the earth to the ends of heaven. . . . Truly I tell you, this generation will not pass away until all these things have taken place." (Mark 13:26–30)

Similar passages appear in Matthew and Luke. The imagery of the Son of Man coming with the clouds is a direct reference to the prophecy from Daniel. In these passages, Jesus assigns a definite time frame to when he will appear as the Son of Man in all his glory. When will it happen? Within a generation, while some of the disciples are still alive.

This thwarts later Christian attempts to explain Jesus' delay by appealing to God's timeline. Even if God sees time differently than we do, it's hard to make the case that "within a generation, while some of the disciples are still alive" can mean something different from God's perspective. More importantly, if Jesus really did teach his disciples that the end would arrive within a single generation, then he proclaimed a major theological falsehood, and this seriously undermines his spiritual authority.

This topic always makes me think of a passage in the Old Testament where Moses explains how to distinguish between real prophets and false ones. He says, "If a prophet speaks in the name of the Lord but the thing does not take place or prove true, it is a word that the Lord has not spoken" (Deuteronomy 18:22). Moses' words seem to cast a dark shadow on Jesus' ministry. If Jesus really predicted that the end of the world would come while some of his disciples were still alive, then he is a false prophet by biblical standards. Christians thus face the challenge of clearing their Lord's name.

This Generation Will Not Pass Away

Some Christians claim that, when Jesus says, "This generation will not pass away until all these things take place," the word translated as "generation" should actually be translated as "race," meaning either the Jewish race in particular or the human race as a whole.[2] However, this doesn't really make sense either in this context or in any other context in the gospels where the word appears. In fact, the Gospel of Matthew contains a genealogy which is broken out into three groups of fourteen "generations," using the same Greek word (Matthew 1:17).

Another theory suggests that when Jesus says "this generation," he is not talking about his own generation, but about the generation that will be alive at the time that these things happen.[3] The problem with this argument is that "this generation" is a recurring phrase in Jesus' teachings, and elsewhere it is abundantly clear that he is referring to his contemporaries (see Mark 8:11–12). In some of the other passages, Jesus seems to envision himself as speaking to the last generation, that is, the final generation before the end of the present age. Notably, Jesus says that "this generation" will be held accountable for "all the righteous blood shed on earth" (Matthew 23:34–36).

Related to this last point, while visiting the temple in Jerusalem, Jesus tells a parable about a man who leases his vineyard to certain tenants, who then refuse to pay him his share of the produce. The man sends his slaves to collect the payment, but the tenants beat or kill them. Finally, the man sends his son, whom the tenants also kill. Jesus ends the parable by saying that the man "will come and destroy the tenants and give the vineyard to others" (Mark 12:1–12).

This parable is meant as a warning to the religious leaders in Jerusalem. The slaves are meant to represent the prophets of old, many of whom were killed, and it is clear that the son is meant to represent Jesus. According to this passage, Jesus sees himself as the last in a succession of messengers before God finally steps in and punishes the "tenants" for their sins. If Jesus is the last messenger, then he must be living in the final generation before that judgment takes place. Because of this, there is no sense in claiming that "this generation" refers to a future generation.

Since there is no getting away from the fact that Jesus is speaking to his own generation, some Christians have argued that when Jesus says "until all these things have taken place," the phrase "all these things" refers to the events preceding the appearance of the Son of Man—wars, persecutions, and the destruction of the temple and Jerusalem—but not the appearance of the Son of Man itself.[4] Of course, if judgment is supposed to come upon "this generation," and if the Son of Man is the one who enacts that judgment, then it would make no sense for Jesus to have expected a gap of thousands of years (or perhaps many more) between the preceding events and the Son of Man's appearance.

It's also clear from the surrounding context that the Son of Man's appearance is supposed to occur immediately after the preceding events:

> In those days, after that suffering, the sun will be darkened, and the moon will not give its light, and the stars will be falling from heaven, and the powers in the heavens will be shaken. Then they will see "the Son of Man coming in clouds" with great power and glory. (Mark 13:24–26)

Notice that Jesus says that this will take place "in those days." He also says that "they will see" the Son of Man. Who are "they"? The people alive at the time "all these things" take place, or in other words, the people of "this generation." So there is no sense in saying that Jesus only meant to assign a time frame to the events preceding the final judgment, but not the final judgment itself.

Some Standing Here Who Will Not Taste Death

What about the other time-sensitive prediction? After talking about the coming of the Son of Man, Jesus says that some of his disciples "will not taste death until they see that the kingdom of God has come with power" (Mark 9:1). To escape the force of Jesus' words, Christians often claim that he is not actually speaking about the establishment of God's kingdom in all its glory. Rather, he is referring to something else that his disciples would live to see, whether his miracles, his resurrection, the coming of the Holy Spirit at Pentecost (see Acts 2:1–13), or Jesus' spiritual reign over the church.[5]

However, this defies the inner logic of Jesus' prediction. When he says, "Some of you will not taste death," the implication is that others of them will. According to the New Testament, Jesus' disciples were not being tortured or put to death prior to his resurrection, the coming of the Holy Spirit, or the emergence of the church. And by this point in the gospel narrative, they were already well-acquainted with his miracles.

But perhaps we have moved too quickly. After Jesus tells his disciples that some of them will not taste death before they see the kingdom of God coming with power, the first three gospels all transition immediately to the story of the transfiguration, which is something that only three of the disciples get to witness. In this story, Peter, James, and John all get to see Jesus momentarily transformed into a state of glory, almost like a preview of things to come (Mark 9:2–8). Presumably, the other disciples would not get to see this until after they died. For this reason, many Christians believe that Jesus' prediction was fulfilled by the transfiguration.

The problem with this view is that it does not take the full context of the saying into account. It's important to note that Jesus' prediction appears at the end of a section where he talks about how the Son of Man will appear with his angels. In fact, Matthew's version of this saying makes it even more clear that Jesus is talking about the moment when the Son of Man will appear in order to carry out God's final judgment:

> For the Son of Man is to come with his angels in the glory of his Father, and then he will repay everyone for what has been done. Truly, I tell you, there are some standing here who will not taste death before they see the Son of Man coming in his kingdom. (Matthew 16:27–28)

Since Jesus relates the coming of the kingdom to the coming of the Son of Man with his angels at the time of the final judgment, there is no meaningful sense in which the transfiguration fits this profile.

The Coming of the Son of Man

It seems pretty clear, then, that in the first three gospels, Jesus expects "the coming of the Son of Man" to take place within a single generation, while some of his disciples are still breathing. But what if "the coming of the Son of Man" is not a reference to the second coming? Some Christians have argued that it is actually a metaphor for the destruction of Jerusalem, and thus for the vindication of Jesus and God's people, since the leaders of Jerusalem had conspired with the Romans to have the Messiah put to death. If this is correct, then Jesus' words really did come true within a generation.

Christians who defend this view still believe in the second coming of Jesus, since the rest of the New Testament talks about it, and they acknowledge that the second coming has not yet taken place. What they deny is that Jesus spoke about the second coming himself. Crucially, this whole theory rests on the assumption that, when Christians in the first century heard about "the Son of Man coming on the clouds of heaven," they would not have connected it to the second coming. Rather, they would have known that it was a metaphor for the destruction of Jerusalem.[6]

However, this underlying assumption is simply false. There are striking parallels between the way the gospels describe the coming of the Son of Man and the way that other New Testament passages describe the second coming of Jesus. Paul speaks of Jesus descending from heaven with the sound of a trumpet and an archangel's call, and of believers being caught up in the clouds to meet Jesus (1 Thessalonians 4:13–18). All of these elements—the clouds, the trumpet, angelic beings, and the gathering together of God's people—are also featured in the gospels' description of the Son of Man's appearance (see especially Matthew 24:30–31).

Additionally, there are several New Testament passages which speak of Jesus returning "like a thief" (1 Thessalonians 5:2; 2 Peter 3:10; Revelation 3:3). This seems to have been a popular Christian image for the second coming. But this image also gets used in connection with the coming of the Son of Man (Matthew 24:43–44; Luke 12:39–40).

The presence of clouds at the appearance of the Son of Man is derived from the prophecy in the book of Daniel (see Daniel 7:13–14). It is significant, then, that the New Testament repeatedly associates the second coming with clouds. We already saw this with Paul, but the book of Revelation also does this by making a direct reference to the prophecy from Daniel, and a few verses later it even describes Jesus as "one like the Son of Man" (Revelation 1:7, 13). Likewise, in the book of Acts, after Jesus ascends to heaven behind a cloud, some angels say, "This Jesus, who has been taken up from you into heaven, will come in the same way as you saw him go into heaven" (Acts 1:11). Given the way that first-century Christians spoke about the second coming and the coming of the Son of Man in such similar terms, connecting both to the prophecy from Daniel, it is clear that they equated the two events.

Sayings Out of Context

At this point we need to take a quick digression. Based on several lines of evidence, including close agreements in wording, it has long been known that there is some kind of literary relationship between the first three gospels. In other words, it's not as if Matthew, Mark, and Luke all just sat down and wrote out their own thoughts and recollections about Jesus. In many cases, they were copying their material directly. It's similar to how we detect plagiarism today.

While some people think that Mark copied from the other two gospels, the vast majority of scholars think that Matthew and Luke copied from Mark, and I think they are right. Otherwise, we'd have to believe that Mark chose to omit all sorts of important material, including the stories of Jesus' birth and vast swaths of his teachings, while making some rather odd choices about what material to add. This added material would include Jesus' family trying to restrain him after some people in the crowd decide that he's out of his mind (Mark 3:19–21), a healing story where Jesus' first attempt at healing isn't fully effective (Mark 8:22–26), and a bizarre detail about an unnamed young man running away naked from the scene of Jesus' arrest (Mark 14:51–52). It seems more likely that Matthew and Luke expanded on Mark by adding in lots of material while removing these other passages. It is also usually thought that Matthew and Luke copied from another source that no longer exists, which scholars call Q.

This has some relevance to the false predictions of Jesus, because one thing we learn from comparing the gospels to each other is that the authors often place the same material in different narrative contexts. For instance, Matthew groups a large amount of Jesus' sayings into a section called the Sermon on the Mount, but in Luke, many of these sayings appear in different sections and are arranged differently. Since the authors felt free to move Jesus' sayings around to suit their own purposes, some Christian apologists have argued that we can't really be sure of what Jesus' time-sensitive predictions meant in their original context, and therefore we should not let them bother us.[7]

Of course, if this argument truly worked, it would undermine our attempts to understand *any* sayings of Jesus, including his apparent claims to divinity, since the same reasoning would apply to all of them. It's true that Jesus' sayings were used by the gospel authors in different ways, and that they placed his teachings in different contexts to make different points. But why should this only become a problem now, when we are dealing with a statement that puts Jesus in a negative light?

Now, there certainly are sayings of Jesus whose original meaning remains obscure. "Let the dead bury their own dead" is a notorious example (see Matthew 8:22). However, the difficulty with that particular saying is that it's hard to know exactly what Jesus meant by "the dead." The surrounding context of his ministry does not shed any conclusive light on the matter. By contrast, there's no getting around the meaning of "this generation" or "the coming of the Son of Man."

Apologists have tried to counter the clear meaning of the predictions by saying that Jesus presupposes a much longer time period before the coming of the Son of Man than a single generation would allow, since he predicts famines, wars, and persecutions. More than that, he predicts that his message will be proclaimed to all nations. Since it would have been impossible for this to happen in his disciples' lifetimes, it can't be what Jesus actually meant.[8]

This argument is oddly self-defeating. It makes no sense to give preferential treatment to Jesus' sayings about wars, famines, and the spread of the gospel if the conclusion is going to be that we can't know what his sayings meant in their original context. If we can't understand his sayings, then why act as if we know what he means when he talks about the events that will precede his appearance as the Son of Man? There's also no reason to assume that, in Jesus' mind, it would take longer than a generation for all these things to happen. Even if *we* happen to think that it would, we can't just assume that a prophet in the ancient Mediterranean world would have agreed with us. In any case, arguing that Jesus can't have meant what he said, because then he would be wrong, is about as question-begging as it gets.

No One Knows the Day or the Hour

There is one last argument for denying the time-sensitive nature of Jesus' predictions, and it's probably the one I heard the most when I was growing up. At one point, Jesus admits that he does not know the exact "day or hour" when his words will finally be fulfilled (Mark 13:32). Christians often cite this verse as proof that Jesus never gave his disciples any reason to expect him to return quickly.

Of course, there's nothing even remotely contradictory about saying, "This will happen in your lifetimes, but I don't know the exact day or hour." The whole point of telling his disciples that no one knows the day or hour is to warn them that it could happen at any moment. This is why, in the verse that immediately follows, Jesus adds, "Beware, keep alert, for you do not know when the time will come" (Mark 13:33). So there's no substance to this argument whatsoever.

Conditional Prophecies

Since there's no reasonable way to get around the fact that Jesus' predictions did not come true, some Christian theologians have proposed a bold alternative hypothesis. They admit that Jesus made time-sensitive predictions, and they also admit that these predictions were not fulfilled. However, they don't consider this to be a problem. Why not? Because they claim that it's okay for an authentic prophet from God to make predictions that don't come true.

This view acknowledges that, according to Moses, if a prophecy doesn't come true, then the prophet was not sent by God (Deuteronomy 18:22). But it points out that many prophecies of God's imminent judgment are conditional, and their fulfillment depends on how humans respond to his message. There are lots of places in the Bible where God changes his mind (for example, Exodus 32:14). So perhaps Jesus' prophecies did not come true because they were conditional, based on human response.[9]

Now, we need not deny that many of the divine promises in the Old Testament are conditional, but the reason we acknowledge them as conditional is, quite simply, because there are conditions written into them (for an example, see Jeremiah 18:7–8). It follows that if a prophet gives people conditions under which they would receive God's blessings, and if they meet those conditions and still don't receive the blessings, then it's a false prophecy. Moses' logic still applies.

The first problem, then, is that Jesus' predictions don't include any conditions. Rather, he predicts that the Son of Man will arrive to carry out the final judgment while some of his contemporaries are still alive. Since this prediction did not come true, his teaching is false, and he is therefore (by Moses' standard) a false prophet.

Another problem is that it wouldn't make sense for the promise of Jesus' imminent return to be conditional in the first place. Conditional prophecies in the Bible operate under the assumption that God is going to punish the wicked and reward the righteous. If people want to avoid the catastrophe that God is planning, they need to repent of their sins (this theme plays a major role in the book of Jonah). But the Son of Man's appearance is not something that Jesus' obedient followers are supposed to be afraid of. The message is not, "Repent, or I'll send the Son of Man to you!" Rather, the Son of Man's appearance is a good thing. Jesus says,

"Now when these things begin to take place, stand up and raise your heads, because your redemption is drawing near" (Luke 21:28).

Likewise, when Paul says, "The God of peace will shortly crush Satan under your feet" (Romans 16:20), this is meant to be an encouragement, not a threat. The early Christians *wanted* Jesus to return and defeat Satan. For them, it would mean the end of their pain and suffering, the end of persecution. In this context, it would be monstrous for God to dangle the hope of an imminent second coming before their minds and hearts, only to take it away for reasons that he had not previously disclosed to them.

Perhaps the biggest problem with explaining an unfulfilled prophecy by saying that God changed his mind is that it empties God's promises of all meaning. If I know that there's always a chance that God will not follow through on his promises, for reasons that have nothing to do with me specifically (say, if not enough people in the world repent), then I no longer have any reason to trust God. I can pray for Jesus to return all I want, and I can follow Jesus' (apparently misguided) advice to prepare myself so that I am ready for the moment. In the end, it will make no difference. God may decide to keep me waiting until I die, just because of something that has nothing to do with me.

In that case, all I can really do is get on with my life and figure out how to live in a way that seems right to me, and maybe someday God will finally put an end to suffering and bring eternal healing to the world. Of course, if I have to go by what seems right to me, it contradicts the idea that I'm supposed to live my life by Jesus' teachings, and it leaves me without any compelling reason to believe in his spiritual authority.

Chapter 3

The Gospels

Up until now we have been treating the gospels as reliable accounts of Jesus' words and deeds, but now we need to stop and reevaluate this assumption. Many Christians, particularly in more liberal church settings, are happy to deny the full historical accuracy of the gospels. Taking a cue from modern biblical scholarship, they cheerfully embrace the claim that the gospel narratives are heavily shaped and influenced by Christian theological concerns. In many cases, they even treat the gospels as metaphorical narratives rather than as historical reports.

This would seem to provide a perfect escape route from having to think of Jesus as a false prophet, since one can simply deny that the time-sensitive prophecies about the Son of Man actually reflect Jesus' authentic teachings. The argument is that these prophecies were invented by the early church and were later written into the gospel narratives as if they were the actual words of Jesus. To know what Jesus really taught, we have to separate the voice of the Christian community from the authentic voice of Jesus. Once we do this, the picture of Jesus that emerges is that of an aphoristic sage, a subversive wisdom teacher, a socially conscious prophet, a Jewish mystic, a gifted healer, a political revolutionary, a spiritual guru, or any number of other possibilities.

If this approach is correct, then we do not need to attribute false teachings to Jesus. However, I don't think this approach actually works, but explaining why it doesn't work is somewhat complicated, since I happen to agree that the gospels contain a blend of history and legend. This means that we have a fair amount of ground left to cover. Our current task is to examine some of the evidence for why the gospels can't be treated as fully reliable sources of historical truth.

The Authors of the Gospels

For much of the church's history, it was almost taken for granted that the four gospels in the New Testament were based on eyewitness testimony. Two of them—the gospels of Matthew and John—were attributed directly to disciples of Jesus. But with the rise of modern biblical scholarship, many traditional views of the Bible's authorship have been called into question. The standard view among scholars today is that the gospels were written by anonymous Christians about forty or more years after the events they record.

To see why most scholars come to this conclusion, we can begin by observing that the authors of the gospels do not name themselves. Their names are given in the titles, but the titles are often thought to have been added to the books at a later stage (more on that later). It is crucial to note that the four gospels are written as objective, third-person accounts, rather than as personal memoirs.

There are only two places in the gospels where the authors refer to themselves. The first is in the prologue to the Gospel of Luke, where the author makes it clear that he is not an eyewitness to Jesus' ministry (Luke 1:1–4). This same author also refers to himself at several points in the book of Acts, which is a sequel to Luke. Although the author does not mention his name, he gives the impression that he was present with Paul for parts of his missionary journeys (for example, Acts 21:1). Scholars continue to debate the legitimacy of these claims, but whatever the case may be, the author does not identify himself, and he did not witness Jesus' words or deeds firsthand.

The second place in the gospels where an author refers to himself is in the last chapter of the Gospel of John, where the author claims to be relying on the direct testimony of one of Jesus' disciples (John 21:24–25). However, the disciple's name is not provided, and the material in this chapter is usually thought to have been added to the book at a later stage, since it is written in a different style from the rest of the book and since the end of chapter 20 reads very naturally as a conclusion. So we are left wondering who the author is, who the unnamed disciple is supposed to be, and what the relationship is between the original Gospel of John and the material found in the final chapter.

Around 180 C.E., a Christian author named Irenaeus speaks about the gospels, and we know that he is talking about the same four books that we currently find in the New Testament because he quotes directly from each of them. Regarding their authorship, Irenaeus reports the following: Matthew produced a gospel for "the Hebrews," in their own language, while Peter and Paul were still alive. After they died, Peter's disciple and interpreter Mark also wrote a gospel based on Peter's preaching. Luke, who was a friend of Paul, wrote a gospel based on Paul's preaching. Finally, John wrote his own gospel.[1]

Irenaeus provides us with the earliest testimony that attributes all four gospels to their traditional authors. But the value of this testimony is questionable. In particular, it's doubtful that Matthew was written before Mark, since Matthew probably used Mark as a source. His traditions about Matthew and Mark seem to come from an earlier Christian writer named Papias. Writing sometime between 130 and 150 C.E., Papias mentions that Matthew wrote the "oracles" in the Hebrew language (which may mean either Hebrew or Aramaic), and that Mark, who was

Peter's interpreter, wrote down everything he remembered from Peter's preaching about Jesus. Papias claims to have gotten these traditions from people who heard them from a group called "the elders" and from men identified as the Lord's disciples.[2]

There has been quite a lot of debate over the reliability of Papias' testimony on this topic. It should be noted that, in at least some cases, we know that Papias passed along traditions of questionable value. For instance, he claimed that Judas Iscariot survived his suicide attempt (referring to the suicide mentioned in Matthew 27:5), after which Judas became so grotesquely engorged that his head was wider than a wagon, and when he eventually died, the discharge was so foul, it could still be smelled almost a century later.[3] In any case, the Gospel of Matthew was originally written in Greek, not Hebrew or Aramaic, so at least on this front, either Papias is talking about a different composition, or his tradition is unreliable.

Other Christian writers prior to Irenaeus quote from the gospels, but they often blend material from different gospels together rather than quoting them precisely, and they do not seem concerned to identify any particular authors. Many times, they simply attribute the material directly to Jesus himself.[4] There is one point in the writings of Justin Martyr where he references material from Mark and possibly attributes it to Peter, but the wording is vague and open to different interpretations (his phrase "in the memoirs of him" could mean "in Peter's memoirs" or "in the memoirs about Jesus").[5] In general, Christian writers from the time before Irenaeus quote the gospels anonymously.

What about the titles? It's important to note that there are no anonymous copies of the gospels in existence. Every surviving manuscript of the gospels—at least, every manuscript that is complete enough to contain a title—reflects the traditional author's name, with no exceptions that I'm aware of. Still, none of these manuscripts are dated prior to the late second century, right around the time when Christian writers were starting to emphasize the distinct identities of the authors.[6]

Sometimes it is argued that, if second-century Christians were just inventing traditions out of thin air, it is unlikely that they would attribute two of the gospels to Mark and Luke rather than directly to the disciples. The point seems reasonable enough. However, we should not overlook the fact that the author of Luke rules himself out as an eyewitness to Jesus' ministry in his prologue, so there was never an option to attribute his book to a disciple anyway.

The truth is, we just don't know exactly how the process played out, so we are forced to rely on guesswork. Those who the defend traditional views for all four gospels have to resort to a heavy amount of speculation and a fairly selective approach to deciding which statements of Papias and Irenaeus are reliable. This only underscores the fact that the authors really do remain unknown to us.

Having said all that, I do not feel very confident about the conventional wisdom that the gospels were all originally published as anonymous books. I also think a good case can be made for the claim that the Gospel of Mark really was written by a man named Mark, though I think it would be impossible to demonstrate a definite connection to the disciple Peter with reasonable confidence.[7]

Furthermore, I have no strong opinion about whether Luke was written by a companion of Paul or whether the author's claim on this matter was an act of forgery (I am open to either possibility).[8] I doubt that Matthew and John composed the gospels bearing their names, but my lack of confidence here stems more from the historical problems involved in trying to treat these books as eyewitness sources and from considerations about their dating (all of which will be discussed shortly).

Nevertheless, it's common practice to refer to all four authors by their traditional names.

Dating the Gospels

In order to understand the issues involved in dating the gospels, it's important to keep in mind that Matthew and Luke copied a significant amount of material from Mark and probably from Q as well. It also helps to remember that Jesus' crucifixion took place around 30 C.E.

We will start with the Gospel of Mark, since it is the earliest gospel. The "end times" discourse in Mark 13 concerns the impending destruction of Jerusalem and its temple, which occurred in the year 70. There is reason to think that the Gospel of Mark was written very close to these events, but scholars mainly disagree on whether the author was writing shortly before the events in question or shortly afterward.

At one point in the discourse, Mark includes a comment made directly to the reader, rather than to Jesus' listeners (see Mark 13:14). This verse encourages those in Judea (where Jerusalem was located) to be ready to flee to the mountains once they see the "desolating sacrilege," which seems to be Mark's way of applying a prophecy from Daniel to the impending desecration of the Jewish temple. Mark's comment to the reader could either be taken as a way of emphasizing something that has just happened or as a call to attention about something that is going to happen very soon. Thus, most scholars see the Gospel of Mark as having been written either in the late 60s or in the early 70s.

Matthew and Luke must be later than that, since they used Mark as a source. We know from quotations in other Christian writings that Matthew was written by the end of the first century. Matthew also contains a saying about a king sending his troops and burning a city

(Matthew 22:7). These words occur in a context where Jesus is criticizing the Jerusalem leadership, and they are usually thought to reflect the author's awareness of Jerusalem's destruction. On the basis of these and certain other details, scholars usually put Matthew in the 80s.

Luke is usually thought to have been written independently of Matthew, meaning that the author was not aware of the other gospel, and this is better explained if Luke was also written in the late first century as opposed to the second century when Matthew was already well known. A significant minority view holds that Acts is dependent on the writings of the Jewish historian Josephus, which would put it (and probably Luke) in the early second century. This actually fits well with another minority theory which holds that Luke used Matthew as a source. But most scholars still see Luke as probably having been written in the 80s, around the same time as Matthew.

The Gospel of John is typically dated to the last decade of the first century. One detail that usually gets mentioned is the gospel's depiction of Jesus' followers being expelled from Jewish synagogues (see John 9:22), which is unlikely to have been the case during Jesus' ministry. It is usually thought to be more reflective of what was happening in the late first century, presumably in the author's own time.

This is reinforced by the material from chapter 21, where the author addresses the fact that Jesus was expected to return before a certain disciple had died. We've seen that the early Christians really did expect Jesus to return in their lifetimes, and that there is material to support this expectation in the other three gospels. Since the Gospel of John strains to deny this, it's plausible to think that the book was published at a time when Christians were starting to cope with the fact that Jesus had not returned yet, and when most or all of Jesus' original followers had died. This fits easily with a late first-century date.

Such are the standard dates given for the gospels. The arguments seem reasonable enough, but they have come under heavy fire from Christian apologetics resources. Apologists often claim that the gospels were written much closer in time to the events they recount. This would seem to increase the historical value of the gospels. So is there any evidence to support the earlier dates?

The Gospel of John contains a few elements that seem to reflect an earlier time period for the writer. Most significantly, there is one passage that seems to treat the Jewish temple as still standing (see John 5:2–3). If this is correct, one would think that it was written prior to Jerusalem's destruction. Yet this feature of John is usually explained by the way the book appears to have been written in stages. I mentioned earlier that chapter 21 is usually thought to be a later addition. Chapters 15–17 also seem like a later addition, since they seem to break the natural flow between the surrounding verses, and they create certain odd discontinuities. Based on these and other signs of editing, the evidence for an earlier dating for John loses much of its force.

In my experience, the most oft-cited evidence for placing the gospels earlier in the first century is the ending of the book of Acts. This book is a narrative concerning the early days of the church, and it reports many of the sufferings faced by the early Christians, even recounting some of their public executions. It is surprising, then, when the book ends with the apostle Paul in prison, awaiting his trial in Rome. Since Paul was probably killed sometime around 64 C.E., the argument is that the author of Acts must not have known about Paul's death, otherwise he surely would have mentioned it. Since he doesn't mention it, he must have been writing in the early 60s. Luke would obviously be earlier than Acts, and Mark would have to be earlier than Luke.

Of course, even if Acts was written after Paul's death, it does not follow that the author *had* to include that in his narrative. Perhaps he was trying to end the story on a positive note. In any case, the Gospel of Luke makes additions to Mark's "end times" discourse that seem to reflect the author's awareness of Jerusalem's destruction. Whereas Mark warns his readers to be ready for the "desolating sacrilege," Luke changes the wording so that his version reads, "When you see Jerusalem surrounded by armies, then know that its desolation has come near." A few verses later, Luke adds another comment about how "Jerusalem will be trampled on by the nations, until the times of the nations are fulfilled" (Luke 21:20–24). The Greek word for "nations" also means "gentiles," and this is probably a reference to the Romans. So there is no good reason to insist on an earlier dating for Luke or Acts.

The Gospels as Ancient Biographies

In some ways, the gospels are a unique type of ancient literature, but scholars generally recognize that they bear a strong resemblance to Greco-Roman biographies. Additionally, the Gospel of Luke and the book of Acts reflect the author's familiarity with Greco-Roman historiography. However, these are not modern biographies, which means it would be a mistake to judge the credibility of the authors by modern standards. Complicating matters further, they are also religious biographies written by people who literally worshiped the subject they were writing about.

At a broad level, all four gospels tell a similar story about Jesus, but when we look at them more closely, we can see lots of differences, especially when different gospels tell the same stories. For example, in Matthew, a Roman centurion approaches Jesus and begs him to heal his servant. After a brief exchange, Jesus heals the servant remotely, without traveling to the centurion's house (Matthew 8:5–13). Luke tells the same story, but in his version, the centurion does not approach Jesus himself. Instead, he sends some Jewish elders to speak to Jesus on his behalf (Luke 7:1–10).

This seems like a straightforward contradiction, but ancient writers did not have to operate by the same standards that contemporary writers do. If a centurion sent Jewish elders to speak to Jesus on his behalf, as Luke says, another writer like Matthew could "compress" the story by telling it as if the centurion had gone to see Jesus himself.[9]

Of course, even if Matthew's writing style is technically legitimate by ancient standards, it still creates a discrepancy, and the point of noting a discrepancy is to call attention to the fact that some detail should not be taken as historically accurate. In other words, if the centurion really did send elders to speak to Jesus on his behalf, then, for the purposes of historical reconstruction, we cannot say that Matthew's version reflects the way things actually happened. Furthermore, while some discrepancies in the gospels can be chalked up to ancient writing styles, others are not so easy to get around. In a number of cases, there is no doubt that the authors made real, conflicting claims about Jesus, implying that at least one of the accounts is wrong.

Contradictions in the Gospels

There are two narratives of Jesus' birth, one in Matthew, the other in Luke. These accounts are significantly different from each other, and in some ways they are incompatible. The major discrepancy has to do with where Jesus' parents were living at the time of his birth. In the Gospel of Luke, Mary and Joseph live in Nazareth, and they travel south to Bethlehem to register for a census (see Luke 2:1–40). By contrast, in the

Gospel of Matthew, they live in Bethlehem at the time of Jesus' birth, and only later do they move to Nazareth (see Matthew 1:18–2:23).

It's true that Matthew never explicitly says "they lived in Bethlehem," but it is clearly implied. One key detail comes up when Jesus' family escapes Herod by fleeing to Egypt. After Herod dies, an angel informs Joseph that they can now return to the land of Israel, because the people who were trying to kill Jesus are dead. Joseph brings his family back to Israel, but when he realizes that Herod's son is now reigning over Judea (where Bethlehem is located), he is afraid to go back there. Instead, he moves his family to the region of Galilee, and they make their home in Nazareth.

This is where all attempts to harmonize the two stories fall apart. If Mary and Joseph already had a home in Nazareth, as Luke says, why would Joseph consider returning to Judea after leaving Egypt? For that matter, why go to Egypt at all? The narrative in Matthew makes no sense unless Mary and Joseph lived in Bethlehem when Jesus was born.

One might try to avoid the contradiction by denying that both stories are meant to be taken literally, but that turns out to be a dead end. Luke's prologue states his intention as a historian pretty clearly by ancient standards, and he attempts to situate Jesus' birth in a historical setting by explaining that it took place during the time of a census imposed on the Roman empire "while Quirinius was governing Syria" (Luke 2:2). Likewise, Matthew repeatedly emphasizes that the events surrounding Jesus' birth happened in order to fulfill biblical prophecies. It seems that both writers took themselves to be reporting on actual events. Thus, at least one of the birth narratives is wrong.

Another example concerns Jesus' interrogation by Pontius Pilate. In the Gospel of Mark, when Jesus appears before Pilate, he says almost nothing. Pilate asks him directly, "Are you the King of the Jews?" to

which Jesus replies, "You say so." Upon further questioning, Jesus remains silent (Mark 15:1–5). That seems to be the entirety of the exchange. However, in the Gospel of John, Jesus answers Pilate's question
differently, and then they have a long dialogue with each other (John
18:33–19:12).

Some apologists claim that Mark is simply compressing the story, but
this theory only works if you ignore Mark's comment that "Jesus made
no further reply." In other words, Mark is not compressing a longer
conversation. Instead, he specifically denies that Jesus had anything more
to say to Pilate. Thus, Mark and John have a genuine disagreement about
what Jesus said to Pilate.

Overstating the Reliability of the Gospels

By this point, we have seen why most scholars treat the gospels as late
first-century sources written by Christians who were not eyewitnesses to
Jesus' ministry. Not surprisingly, many Christian apologists have labored
hard to defend the historical credibility of the gospels. Of course, since
the gospels present Jesus as making false theological claims, these efforts
are somewhat self-defeating, but never mind that. Let's consider some of
their arguments.

Since scholars typically put the gospels in the late first century, this
would still potentially be within the lifetimes of eyewitnesses to the
words and deeds of Jesus. Some apologists have argued that, even with
the standard dates, the authors of the gospels could never have gotten away with telling false or exaggerated stories about Jesus, since the
surviving witnesses would have shut them down.[10] Notice that, if this
simple argument actually worked, it would require a complete overhaul
of prevailing New Testament scholarship. But does it work?

Not quite. Even at a theoretical level, this argument for the historical integrity of the gospels is hopelessly naive. It is all too easy for false information to spread about a subject while living witnesses do their best to stop it. Think of all the people who claimed that the Sandy Hook school shooting was a hoax, who were so successful in gaining an audience for their false views that it ruined the lives of parents whose children were killed in the massacre.[11] Have the apologists never heard of Holocaust deniers?

The fact that the gospels were written within a generation or two of Jesus' death is thus insufficient for establishing their historical reliability. Legends about Jesus could have spread quite quickly, even while he was still alive, especially if he was anywhere near as popular as the gospels make him out to be. There are numerous examples in history of legends circulating about notable people shortly after their deaths or during their lifetimes, including people like Alexander the Great, Sabbatai Sevi, George Washington, and Davy Crockett.[12]

The next line of argument is far more subtle. Apologists frequently appeal to the discrepancies in the gospels as evidence for their reliability. They claim that when two gospels disagree with each other, it shows that the authors are not colluding together. This is true, of course, but then the apologists go one step further and say that this lack of collusion proves that the authors can be treated as independent witnesses.[13] Here I want to ask: witnesses to what, exactly? Somehow, the fact that two writers disagree is supposed to show that they are not just making the story up. Yet this argument doesn't work unless it's very carefully nuanced.

Think about the birth narratives. Even on a conservative Christian view, Matthew and Luke were not eyewitnesses to Jesus' birth. At the very least, they are one step (and possibly many steps) removed from the events they are reporting on. The two writers are independent in the sense that they are not copying each other, but this does not automatically mean that they are just giving us the facts.

We've already seen that Matthew and Luke disagree about where Jesus' parents lived at the time of his birth. So which detail in their narratives is this supposed to vindicate as rock-solid historical truth? At least one of their stories must be false to a considerable degree, which means that someone—one of the authors or one of their underlying sources—*did* make something up, whether knowingly or not. If this happened in one case, there's no reason why it couldn't have happened in both cases. So how can the fact that they disagree with each other somehow prove that either one of them is a reliable witness?

Now, there is a germ of truth hidden somewhere in this argument, but it needs to be properly stated. When two sources both attest to the same alleged fact, and if we know they are independent of each other (meaning that neither author is getting their information from the other), it shows that neither one of them is making that detail up. Rather, they must each be getting that detail from an earlier source. This increases the probability that the information is reliable. However, an increase in probability does not necessarily mean that the probability is high enough to establish confidence, since there may still be other factors which weigh against the reliability of the information.

In the birth narratives, Matthew and Luke agree on a few details: the names of Jesus' parents, the virginal conception, the accompaniment of some kind of angelic announcement, the occurrence of Jesus' birth in Bethlehem, and Jesus' being raised in Nazareth. The fact that neither author took this information from the other indicates that these details were probably already part of a tradition concerning Jesus' birth before Matthew and Luke ever set pen to papyrus.

But even though Matthew and Luke are each drawing from earlier traditions, this does not mean that every point of agreement must be taken as fact. As we'll see later, Jesus probably did come from Nazareth, and this fact, coupled with some other important information, actually casts doubt on the claim that he was born in Bethlehem. So while the evidence of "multiple, independent attestation" is important and helpful, it is not a skeleton key that unlocks the door to an indisputable set of historical truths about Jesus. There are lots of different factors that come into play. Each claim about Jesus must be judged by its own merits.

Many apologists also like to treat the differences in the gospels as proof that they are not just copying each other. But we already know that, in many cases, the authors *are* copying from other sources. To repeat a point from earlier, it's not as if four people just sat down and wrote their own individual recollections of Jesus. In other words, they were not composing personal memoirs.

As I mentioned earlier, Matthew and Luke copied a significant amount of material from Mark and Q. I should clarify here that Q is a hypothetical source (that is, it no longer exists, if it ever existed at all), and it is usually thought to be the source of the common material in Matthew and Luke that does not come from Mark. But even Mark and John are usually thought to have copied material from other sources as well. Since the gospels are all borrowing material from earlier sources, it becomes much more difficult to treat them as straightforward eyewitness narratives.

Correcting the Gospel of Mark

If Matthew was a disciple of Jesus, one naturally wonders why he would lean so heavily on a source that was written by someone like Mark, who wasn't an eyewitness. This seems to cast doubt on the traditional views of authorship, but apologists like to argue that, while Matthew was a disciple, he wasn't as close to Jesus as Peter was. Since the Gospel of Mark is allegedly based on the testimony of Peter, we're supposed to think that Matthew would naturally have prioritized the material in Mark over his own personal experience.[14]

To see why this theory doesn't make sense, we can begin by observing several instances where Matthew intentionally changes his source material from Mark. For example, there are a few places in Mark where Jesus is described as getting angry (Mark 3:5; 10:14; and probably 1:41).[15] Parallels for all these verses appear in both Matthew and Luke, and in every single case, the authors remove the reference to Jesus' anger. We can understand the omissions, since Jesus taught his disciples that "if you are angry with a brother or sister, you will be liable to judgment" (Matthew 5:22). Matthew and Luke are presenting a picture of Jesus that falls better in line with Christian beliefs. But they do this by distorting their source material.

For another example, consider the story of Jesus walking on water. According to the story, the disciples have just witnessed an incredible event: Jesus' miraculous feeding of five thousand people with only five loaves of bread and two fish. Afterward, he tells the disciples to get in their boat and go ahead of him to a town called Bethsaida. Later that night, still in the boat, the disciples are caught in a storm and struggling against the wind. At that moment, they see Jesus walking on the water. Thinking that he is a ghost, they begin to panic, but then Jesus gets in the boat and the storm stops. Mark ends this story by saying, "And they were utterly astounded, for they did not understand about the loaves, but their hearts were hardened" (Mark 6:45–52).

Matthew copies this story from Mark, but he takes out the part about the disciples' hardened hearts, replacing it with, "And those in the boat worshiped him saying, 'Truly you are the Son of God'" (Matthew 14:22–33). Quite a turnaround for the disciples!

At another point in Mark's narrative, Jesus teaches at the synagogue in his hometown, but the people there take offense at him. Mark ends the story by saying, "And he could do no deed of power there, except that he laid his hands on a few sick people and cured them. And he was amazed at their unbelief" (Mark 6:5–6). This seems to suggest a limitation of Jesus' power. However, when Matthew retells this story, he changes the wording. His version simply says, "And he did not do many deeds of power there, because of their unbelief" (Matthew 13:58). Now the lack of miracles stems from a choice Jesus made in response to the people's lack of faith.

Matthew is even willing to change Jesus' words if it suits his purposes. In one story, as told by Mark, a young man approaches Jesus to ask him, "Good teacher, what must I do to inherit eternal life?" Jesus replies, "Why do you call me good? No one is good but God alone" (Mark 10:17-18). Jesus seems to be denying his own perfect goodness, which would imply a denial of his divinity. At least, it's easy to read the passage that way. In Matthew's version, the man asks Jesus, "Teacher, what good deed must I do to have eternal life?" to which Jesus replies, "Why do you ask me about what is good? There is one who is good" (Matthew 19:16-17). It seems that Matthew has changed the wording of both speakers in order to avoid a theological difficulty.

When I was growing up in the church, we treated all four gospels as if they were written to be read side by side. We took for granted that the different accounts were meant to complement each other. But the fact that Matthew and Luke changed their material from Mark suggests that they never intended for their books to be read alongside each other. By changing their source material, it seems that the authors were actually trying to provide a superior, more authoritative account of events (and Luke's prologue directly supports this idea). This works against the theory that Matthew was an eyewitness who nevertheless relied on Mark because he was not as close to Jesus as Peter was.

The Gospel of John

The differences between Matthew and Mark pale in comparison to the differences between John and the other three gospels. It's true that all four gospels tell a similar basic story, but John's narrative framework is strikingly different from that of the other gospels, in at least five ways.

First, the Gospel of John contains no exorcisms. This is surprising, because the other gospels are filled with reports of Jesus casting out demons, and Jesus attaches major significance to his ministry as an exorcist (see Luke 11:20). Second, in John's account, Jesus performs many "signs" of his divine authority so that other people can believe in him. However, in the other three gospels, Jesus explicitly refuses to perform signs when asked (Mark 8:12).

Third, in the first three gospels, Jesus does not tend to speak openly about his identity. In the Gospel of Mark, he never directly claims to be the Messiah until he is on trial before the Judean council. By contrast, in the Gospel of John, Jesus speaks openly, publicly, and at great length about his divine nature and his identity as the Messiah. Fourth, a central theme of Jesus' teachings in the first three gospels is the kingdom of God. It's a topic that Jesus returns to frequently. However, this theme is almost entirely absent from the Gospel of John.

Finally, Jesus' teachings in the first three gospels mainly consist of short sayings and parables. Even the longer discourses, such as the Sermon on the Mount, usually consist of a series of shorter sayings. However, in the Gospel of John, Jesus speaks in long monologues, and he does not tell any parables. Whereas the parables in the other gospels make heavy use of similes ("The kingdom of God is like..."), the discourses in John are based on metaphors ("I am the good shepherd," "I am the true vine," etc.).

In addition to these major differences in the narrative framework, the Gospel of John also presents a much more powerful, idealized portrait of Jesus than what we find in the other gospels:

- In the first three gospels, Jesus pleads with God to spare him from the suffering that he knows he must endure (Mark 14:36). But in the Gospel of John, Jesus explicitly repudiates the idea of making such a prayer (John 12:27).

- In the first three gospels, when the crowd shows up at Gethsemane to arrest Jesus, Judas Iscariot identifies Jesus for them by greeting him with a kiss, which was a normal way to greet someone and which was probably meant as a way to identify Jesus without arousing his suspicion (Mark 14:43–46). However, in the Gospel of John, Jesus identifies himself to the crowd. He apparently speaks with such authority that it causes the crowd to step back and fall to the ground (John 18:3–8).

- In the first three gospels, after Jesus is sentenced to death, someone else is forced to carry his cross (Mark 15:21). By contrast, the Gospel of John explicitly says that Jesus carried the cross "by himself" (John 19:17).

- As noted earlier, in the first three gospels, when Jesus appears before Pontius Pilate, he says almost nothing to him. However, in the Gospel of John, he engages in a full dialogue with him, and he speaks openly and authoritatively about his kingdom.

Apologists tend to focus on these issues in a piecemeal fashion, offering elaborate interpretive strategies in an attempt to show that a particular verse from one gospel does not decisively contradict a particular verse from another. But when we look at these issues together, it is hard not to see that John has a consistent pattern of making Jesus seem more authoritative and powerful than he appears to be in the earlier gospels.

Since John shows a repeated pattern of heightening or exaggerating Jesus' power and authority beyond what we find in the other gospels, it's very difficult to think that John's gospel is nothing more than the personal recollections of one of Jesus' disciples. Something else is going on here. We are dealing with drastically different perspectives on the sort of person Jesus was.

Against all of this, apologists sometimes like to point out that in a brief passage from Q, Jesus speaks about his unique relationship to God in a manner that is strangely reminiscent of the way he speaks in the Gospel of John:

> All things were given to me by my Father, and no one knows the Son except the Father, nor does anyone know the Father except the Son and those to whom the Son wishes to reveal him. (Matthew 11:27; Luke 10:22)

Sometimes this passage is called the "Johannine thunderbolt," since it seems to suddenly drop an element of John's style, out of the blue, into a narrative where this style is otherwise absent. Because of this striking similarity, it is taken by many Christians to confirm that John's portrait of Jesus is grounded in history.[16]

However, this argument is severely overstated. How would a single short saying from Q prove that Jesus really spoke in long metaphorical discourses on a regular basis? How would it prove that he spoke openly and frequently about his divine identity? How would it explain John's lack of exorcisms or dearth of references to the kingdom of God? How would it overturn the fact that John lionizes Jesus? It's hard to see how the Johannine thunderbolt resolves any of these issues.

The Death of Jesus

For an especially compelling argument against treating the gospels as eyewitness sources, we can consider the way that they narrate Jesus' final moments. In the Gospel of Mark, Jesus does not say much once he is up on the cross. After about six hours, he cries out, "My God, my God, why have you forsaken me?" (Mark 15:34). Then he lets out another loud cry before he finally dies. Matthew's narrative is fully in line with Mark on these points.

However, Luke and John both change the story, albeit in different ways, so that Jesus comes across as much calmer and more composed in the face of death. Both of them have him engaging in short exchanges with other people while he hangs on the cross. They also omit Jesus' anguished words about being forsaken by God. Instead, in Luke's account, Jesus says, "Father, into your hands I commend my spirit" (Luke 23:32–47). And in John's account, when Jesus dies on the cross, rather than crying out with a loud voice, he simply says, "It is finished," and then he bows his head and gives up his spirit (John 19:18–30). There is no sense at all of Jesus being abandoned by God. He is fully in control of what's happening to him.

If all four accounts of Jesus' death are historically accurate, we have to think that each gospel is only giving a partial report of his final moments. For this theory to work, we would have to assume that, when Jesus died on the cross, he was both overcome with despair (per Mark and Matthew) and somehow calm and composed at the same time (per Luke and John). Possibly, one can imagine someone experiencing a range of emotions while suffering the brutality of crucifixion, but it is surely impossible to exhibit both extreme despair and extreme calm precisely at the moment of death. The combined narrative seems incoherent.

We would also have to assume that the testimonies of those who witnessed Jesus' death somehow resulted in completely different streams of oral tradition. According to the tradition that ended up in Mark, Jesus was only known to have suffered agony and despair on the cross; according to two other traditions, Jesus was known to have been calm and composed. But why would eyewitness accounts have split off from each other so neatly in this respect?

Apologists sometimes go to absurd lengths to get around this problem. For instance, at one point while Jesus is on the cross in the Gospel of John, he says, "I am thirsty" (John 19:28). Since Jesus speaks elsewhere in this gospel about how God provides his people with "living water," some apologists have argued that when Jesus declares his thirst on the cross, he must really be declaring his sense of spiritual emptiness. Thus, uttering the phrase "I am thirsty" is actually the same thing as screaming "My God, my God, why have you forsaken me?"[17]

As an argument for the historical credibility of the Gospel of John, this theory strikes me as quite ludicrous. Even if it worked, John's crucifixion scene would still be a far cry from what we find in the earlier gospels. John presents Jesus as approaching his death in a calm and composed manner, contrary to the testimony of Mark and Matthew. Notice that this fits perfectly with the way that John lionizes Jesus throughout his whole gospel. Given the rest of John's narrative, it would be utterly jarring for Jesus to suddenly cry out in despair on the cross. Yet according to the eyewitness theory, all of these details must somehow fit together.

What really undermines the attempt to treat these narratives as four complementary eyewitness accounts is Luke. If Luke used Mark as a source, then he is not merely preserving a different report of what happened at Jesus' death. Since Luke was familiar with Mark's version of events, he must have made an intentional decision to alter the story in order to portray Jesus in a strikingly different way.

It's no use saying that Luke was merely trying to complement Mark's version, as if he expected both gospels to be read side by side. We already know that he had no reservations about incorporating over half of Mark's gospel into his own narrative. If he was willing to copy Mark in so many other places, why not here? We can't just pretend not to notice the way that Luke replaces Jesus' despair over being abandoned by God with a calm prayer of submission to his heavenly father. When apologists insist that these accounts are fully compatible, they are asking us to deny what we can see with our own eyes.

Jesus and Jewish Food Laws

Since Mark is the earliest surviving gospel, we are not in a good position to know exactly how he changed his own source material. In spite of this limitation, there are good reasons to think that he changed his material to some degree in order to make it conform to his own theological vision. This casts significant doubt on the idea that Mark is providing a straightforward eyewitness record of Jesus' ministry, much less one that stems directly from the testimony of Peter.

An excellent case in point comes from Mark's account of a conflict between Jesus and the Pharisees (found in Mark 7:1–23). The trouble starts when the Pharisees notice that Jesus' disciples are eating with unwashed hands. For context, the Pharisees were a Jewish group in the first century known for their commitment to ritual purity. They were experts in the Jewish law and developed a body of traditions that, in theory, were meant to assist in helping people obey the law.

When the Pharisees see Jesus' disciples eating with unwashed hands, their concern is not with physical cleanliness, but with ritual purity. The Jewish law prescribes the washing of hands and wooden bowls under certain circumstances for the sake of remaining pure before God (Leviticus 15:11–12). Mark claims that it was a custom among the Pharisees and among "all the Jews" to wash their hands before eating food purchased in the market. Note the implication here that Mark is not writing for a Jewish audience.

The Pharisees confront Jesus on this matter, saying, "Why do your disciples not walk according to the tradition of the elders but eat with defiled hands?" In response, Jesus denounces them as hypocrites, accuses them of abandoning the commandments of God for the sake of tradition, and cites an example related to honoring one's parents. Then he tells the crowd, "Listen to me, all of you, and understand: there is nothing outside a person that by going in can defile, but the things that come out are what defile" (Mark 7:14). Later on, Jesus explains what he means by "things that come out" of a person: "For it is from within, from the human heart, that evil intentions come," by which he means things like murder, wickedness, and debauchery (Mark 7:21–22).

Before going further with Mark's story, we need to take note of two things. First, the Jewish law sets down a number of dietary restrictions in which God differentiates between clean and unclean foods (these can be found in Leviticus 11:1–47 and Deuteronomy 14:3–20). Again, this has nothing to do with physical health or cleanliness, but with ritual purity.

Second, our cultural context plays an important role in how we determine the meaning of an ancient text, and in this case, it can lead us astray. Most scholars think that Jesus really did make the claim that "there is nothing outside a person that by going in can defile, but the things that come out are what defile."[18] If Jesus really said this, it is easy to think (in fact, it seems quite obvious) that Jesus is at odds with the Jewish law, which certainly does teach that some foods can make a person unclean.

However, in an ancient Jewish context, to say, "Not [this], but [that]," could often mean, "Not only [this], but *especially* [that]!"[19] There are examples of this in the Old Testament:

> For in the day that I brought your ancestors out of the land of Egypt, I did not speak to them or command them concerning burnt offerings and sacrifices. But this command I gave them, "Obey my voice, and I will be your God, and you shall be my people." (Jeremiah 7:22–23)

Taken at face value, these words would be hilariously out of touch with the rest of the Old Testament, which depicts God as giving the Israelites' ancestors lots of commands about burnt offerings and sacrifices. However, the passage from Jeremiah simply means that God's faithfulness to his people comes *not just* through observance of the sacrificial system *but also, and especially,* through obedience to God's moral commands. Likewise, in Hoses 6:6 when God says, "I desire steadfast love and not sacrifice," this means that God desires steadfast love much more than sacrifice.

So, when Jesus says that a person is defiled not by what goes into them, but by what comes out of them (that is, out of their heart), he can be understood as saying that one is not just defiled by eating unclean food, but much more by the evil things that come from within them, like murder and hatred.

However, this is not the whole story. Jewish food laws actually became a notable source of conflict in the early Christian community. Contrary to what is written in the law, Paul (who was Jewish himself) flat out denies that anything is "unclean in itself" (Romans 14:14).

So the question is, should we understand Jesus' words as making use of a common form of ancient Jewish rhetoric, or should we take his words at face value? In other words, did Jesus teach his disciples that nothing could make them unclean by going into their bodies, or did he just mean that the evil that comes from inside a person's heart is a much bigger deal than consuming something that is defiled? The answer to this makes a big difference in our understanding of how Jesus viewed the Jewish law. And as it turns out, Mark and Matthew disagree sharply on this point.

In Mark's narrative, after Jesus tells the crowd about what makes a person unclean, he elaborates on his words while speaking privately to his disciples. And there are two details in the account which show that, according to Mark, Jesus should be understood as supporting the view held by Paul. First, he has Jesus state his position more clearly: "Do you not see that whatever goes into a person from outside cannot defile, since it enters not the heart but the stomach and goes out into the sewer?" Second, Mark notes that by saying this, Jesus "declared all foods clean" (Mark 7:17–23). There is no ambiguity here.

However, when Matthew copies the story of Jesus' conflict with the Pharisees over hand washing, he makes some interesting changes (see Matthew 15:1–20). First, he omits Jesus' private comment that "whatever goes into a person from outside cannot defile." Second, he omits Mark's claim that Jesus declared all foods clean. These changes are not inconsequential, because they create space for interpreting Jesus' words more in the spirit of the "not [this] but [that]" rhetorical device.

Furthermore, when we look at what else Jesus says in Matthew's gospel, the difference with Mark is more striking:

> Do not think that I have come to abolish the Law or the Prophets; I have come not to abolish but to fulfill. For truly I tell you, until heaven and earth pass away, not one letter, not one stroke of a letter, will pass from the law until all is accomplished. Therefore, whoever breaks one of the least of these commandments and teaches others to do the same will be called least in the kingdom of heaven, but whoever does them and teaches them will be called great in the kingdom of heaven (Matthew 5:17–19).

It seems, then, that Matthew and Mark are at odds with each other concerning Jesus' attitude toward the law. But there is one more point of tension between the two writers. In Mark's account, Jesus' answer to the Pharisees does not actually address their question. After accusing the Pharisees of hypocrisy, Jesus focuses his attention on food cleanliness. Yet their question to him had nothing to do with food per se. Rather, they asked him why his disciples don't wash their hands before eating. Jesus seems to come off as completely misunderstanding what the Pharisees are asking him.

Matthew resolves this problem quite nicely by adding a comment that does not appear in Mark. He ends the story by having Jesus tell his disciples that "to eat with unwashed hands does not defile" (Matthew 15:20). This does not pose any challenge to the Jewish law, because even though Moses commanded hand washing in certain circumstances, to wash hands specifically before eating was a tradition that came later. More importantly, it adds a bit of coherence to the story that was lacking in Mark's version.

Mark's story about the conflict over hand washing also puts him at odds with Luke. We can begin by observing that Luke omits the story of the conflict altogether. Now, by itself, this proves nothing. But the author of Luke also includes a scene in the book of Acts where Peter receives a vision from God in which he is commanded to eat "unclean" animals because nothing that God creates can really be unclean. As a result of the vision, Peter comes to realize that God's salvation is open to the gentiles (Acts 10:1–11:18).

Now this is interesting for several reasons. First, we must ask why such a vision would even be necessary if Peter already knew that Jesus had declared all foods clean—especially if Peter really was the source behind Mark's gospel narrative. And why would Peter object to the vision commanding him to eat?

Furthermore, how does this all mesh with Paul's account of his conflict with Peter? Paul passionately believed that gentile converts to Christianity should not be made to follow Jewish food laws and that, within the Christian community, Jews and gentiles should have table fellowship together. Peter seems to have gone along with this practice until some of James' men showed up, at which point Peter pulled back from the gentiles (Galatians 2:11–14). This is harder to explain if Peter knew that

Jesus himself had declared all foods clean, or if God had already given him the vision recorded in Acts.

Lest we get bogged down by all these interesting tensions, let's clearly state the biggest disagreement between Mark and Luke on this score. Whereas Mark attributes the rejection of Jewish food laws directly to Jesus during his ministry, Luke attributes it to an event taking place after Jesus' death. Luke would thus seem to agree with Matthew that Jesus did not declare all foods clean, even though they would apparently disagree on whether the food laws were still binding.

All of this wreaks havoc on any attempt to treat the gospels as complimentary eyewitness accounts. More importantly, it shines a spotlight on the fact that Mark is getting just as creative with his source material as Matthew and Luke get with theirs.

The Gospels and History

Clearly the authors of the gospels are not just preserving the direct eyewitness testimony of Jesus' disciples. Rather, they change details to serve their narrative purposes, and they exaggerate and distort the stories of Jesus, sometimes to a striking degree, and often in the service of a theological agenda. They also contradict each other in many ways, which means that at least some of the authors must be getting a number of important details wrong.

As a result, we cannot just assume, in any particular instance, that the gospels are giving us reliable information about Jesus. Every claim needs to be critically evaluated, and some claims will need to be rejected. And why should this surprise us? After all, we are dealing with sacred biographies written by people who literally worshiped the person they were writing about. It would be more surprising if these books did *not* contain any important falsehoods.

It seems that there may be hope, then, for the Christian who wants to deny that Jesus made any time-sensitive predictions. Of course, it comes at a price: one can no longer appeal to the gospels as a reliable authority for spiritual truth. Instead, the gospels only serve as a representation of how Jesus was understood (or misunderstood) by Christians in the first century. If we want to know who Jesus really was, we have to sift through the legendary material and try to discern the historical reality that lay underneath. However, once we do this, we will see that the argument against Jesus' spiritual authority reasserts itself in a powerful way.

Chapter 4

What Jesus Believed

The gospels are not eyewitness accounts; they are religious biographies that blur the line between history and legend to a considerable degree. Yet they are still our best sources for learning who Jesus was. This is a standard view in New Testament scholarship, having nothing to do with commitments to Christian beliefs. It's mainly because these gospels are the earliest accounts of Jesus' ministry that we have, since they were all written in the first century C.E.

By contrast, the gospels outside of the New Testament date to the second century or later. Some scholars put a lot of weight on the Gospel of Thomas, but if I've understood them correctly, even they still usually recognize that the version of Thomas that we have is from the second century. They simply think that it makes use of earlier traditions, and some would argue that these earlier traditions predate the stories in the New Testament gospels. Whether this conclusion has any merit depends in large part on what we do with the gospels in the New Testament.

Searching for Historical Truth in the Gospels

Even though the gospels in the New Testament are full of unreliable details, there are good reasons to think that the authors didn't just invent the story of Jesus out of thin air. Consider the claim that Jesus had a brother named James. This is reported in the Gospel of Mark (Mark

6:3) and also in one of Paul's letters (Galatians 1:19). Paul couldn't have copied from Mark, since Mark was written later, and in any case, we've already seen that Paul was directly acquainted with James. Mark also wasn't getting his information from Paul, since he names other siblings besides James. Interestingly, the first-century historian Josephus also claims that Jesus had a brother named James. In fact, Josephus reports on James' martyrdom, which is not something that is found anywhere in the New Testament.[1] So the likelihood that Jesus had a brother named James is very high (this is one of many reasons why there's no sense in denying that Jesus existed).

One of the most firmly-established facts about Jesus is his death by crucifixion. Numerous Christian sources report that he was crucified, in spite of the fact that these sources also regard him as the Messiah. This is important because we know that the Messiah was widely expected to be some kind of deliverer, someone who would lead God's people to victory. A dead Messiah would be bad enough, but crucifixion was a particularly gruesome and devastating form of death. By design, crucifixion was meant to instill fear in people by reminding them of who was really in charge. In Jesus' world, it was a punishment mainly reserved for the lower classes and non-citizens, especially slaves and political rebels. For this reason, the concept of a crucified Messiah was almost a contradiction in terms. This is why Paul has to defend the idea in spite of its apparent absurdity (see 1 Corinthians 1:18–25).

Of course, we know why Christians continued to believe that Jesus was the Messiah even after he was crucified: they were convinced that God had raised him back to life. It was only in light of their belief in his resurrection that they were able to embrace his crucifixion. Still, the fact that their Messiah had been crucified did not make it any easier for them to win converts. To the outside world, and especially to the rest of the Jewish community, Jesus' crucifixion was an obstacle to faith. If Christians were making the whole story up, they almost certainly would not have said that their Messiah was crucified, since it made them a target for ridicule.

Another solid fact about Jesus is that he came from Nazareth, in the region of Galilee. Many of his Jewish contemporaries were expecting the Messiah to come from Bethlehem because of a prophecy in the Old Testament (see Micah 5:2). Since Jesus was known to have come from Nazareth, this could potentially be seen as a reason to doubt his identity as the Messiah, something that is directly acknowledged in the Gospel of John (see John 7:40–42). The challenge, then, was to explain how Jesus could be from Bethlehem even though he was known to have come from Nazareth.

We've already seen that Matthew and Luke each get Jesus to Bethlehem for his birth, and that they each have their own explanation for how he ended up in Nazareth. And now we can understand why they tell these stories: they're trying to demonstrate Jesus' credibility as the Messiah. While this raises questions about whether Jesus was really born in Bethlehem, it also indicates that Christians didn't invent the fact that he was from Nazareth.

Going a bit further, there's no good reason to doubt that Jesus was Jewish. His first followers were Jewish, he was from Nazareth, his followers interpreted him in Jewish theological terms, and his brother was James, who became a well-known Jewish Christian leader. Not only that, but multiple sources in the gospels portray Jesus as someone who saw his own ministry as somehow fulfilling God's promises in Jewish scripture.

It would be interesting to work through all the other basic facts about Jesus that we can reasonably affirm by carefully studying the evidence, but this book is not meant to be a biography of Jesus. So instead, we will turn our attention to a more pressing question: did Jesus teach his disciples that the end of the age was imminent? There are compelling reasons to think that he did.

The Sayings Material

We can begin by observing the great number of relevant sayings that are attributed to Jesus. We've already looked at two of his predictions, where he says that some of his disciples will not taste death before they see the kingdom of God coming with power, and that the current generation will not pass away until the Son of Man appears. However, there is one more prediction to consider.

Even though Matthew reproduces Mark's "end times" discourse, he also takes some of the material from that discourse and places it in an earlier section where Jesus sends out his twelve disciples to proclaim the good news to different towns (specifically, material from Mark 13:9–13 appears in Matthew 10:17–22). For some reason Matthew thought this was the appropriate place for Jesus to warn his disciples about how someday they will be persecuted for their faith in him. At the end of this section, Matthew adds a line that is not found anywhere else: "When they persecute you in this town, flee to the next, for truly I tell you, you will not have finished going through all the towns of Israel before the Son of Man comes" (Matthew 10:23).

This passage undeniably raises difficult questions. For instance, why would Matthew place this material here? And doesn't this prediction stand in tension with the idea that the gospel must be proclaimed to all nations before the end comes? In spite of these puzzles, the prediction here seems to mesh well with the other two predictions. It even reproduces the same sentence structure: the phrase "truly I tell you," followed by a statement about what will *not* happen, then a temporal conjunction ("before/until"), and finally a statement referring to the end-related event.[2] So this type of prediction is independently attested by Mark and Matthew.

Another source, Q, also has Jesus predicting that "this generation" will be held accountable for all the righteous blood shed on earth (see Matthew 23:34–35; Luke 11:49–50). This provides further independent attestation of Jesus' explicit predictions about the end being near.

In addition to these predictions, the gospels attribute a mass of sayings to Jesus in which he engages with ideas that were often associated in Jewish theology with an imminent end. These themes include conflict with Satan and the demonic realm, the day of judgment (sometimes just called "that day" or "the last day"), the resurrection of the dead, the time of coming suffering or tribulation, and hell as a fiery place of punishment for the wicked after they die.

Another relevant theme, which is attested in multiple, independent sources, is that of the end coming suddenly or unexpectedly. This theme comes up in numerous passages from the first three gospels (for example, Mark 13:32–37). It even comes up in the Gospel of Thomas (verse 21). Why does this matter? Because it wouldn't make sense for Jesus to have talked this way unless he really thought the final judgment would take place soon. There would be something profoundly disjointed about saying, "Keep watch! Be alert! The end will come suddenly, thousands of years from now!"

It doesn't follow that every relevant saying is necessarily authentic. However, if different sources consistently depict Jesus as speaking on these themes, then there's a greater probability that they came up in his actual teachings.

From John the Baptist to the Early Church

Some of the most compelling evidence concerning Jesus' attitude toward the future does not even involve his recorded sayings. To begin with, the expectation of a quickly-approaching final judgment was one of the defining features of the movement that he started. We already looked at the evidence for this in chapter 2. One plausible explanation for why the early Christians clung so tenaciously to this belief is that they were taught to do so by Jesus himself.

And then there's John the Baptist. All four gospels present John's ministry as a precursor to the ministry of Jesus. John's nickname stems from the fact that his ministry involves a baptism of repentance for the forgiveness of sins, and he sees himself as playing an important role in preparing the people for the arrival of another figure who will have great authority:

> The one who is more powerful than I is coming after me;
> I am not worthy to stoop down and untie the strap of his
> sandals. I have baptized you with water, but he will baptize
> you with the Holy Spirit. (Mark 1:7–8)

The first three gospels contain a scene in which John baptizes Jesus in the Jordan river. After this, the heavens open and the Holy Spirit descends on Jesus like a dove. In the Gospel of Mark, a voice from heaven speaks to Jesus and says, "You are my Son, the Beloved; with you I am well pleased" (Mark 1:4–11). Sometime after Jesus' baptism, John is arrested by Herod and thrown in prison. In Matthew and Mark, Jesus does not begin his public ministry until after this happens. While in prison, John sends two of his own disciples to ask Jesus if he is "the one who is to come." After the two disciples leave, Jesus speaks very highly of John (Matthew 11:2–19; Luke 7:18–35).

Jesus' baptism by John is widely accepted as a fact. It's hard to imagine Christians inventing a story where the man they worship participates in a baptism of repentance. Not only that, but the fact that Jesus was baptized by John, and that he admired John even though John was uncertain about him, could be taken to mean that John was spiritually superior to Jesus in some way. The early Christians seem to have struggled with this, which would explain certain details that we find in the gospels.

In Matthew's version of the baptism story, John already knows that Jesus is the person whose coming he has been proclaiming. John says, "I need to be baptized by you, and do you come to me?" Jesus replies, "Let it be so now, for it is proper for us in this way to fulfill all righteousness." Then, when the voice speaks from heaven, it speaks to John and the others present, rather than directly to Jesus (Matthew 3:13–17). Matthew obviously wants to make it clear that Jesus' baptism does not imply his inferiority to John. He also wants to subvert the idea that John didn't know what to make of Jesus.

The Gospel of Luke takes things a bit further by claiming that John and Jesus were actually cousins, whose births were both surrounded by miraculous circumstances in which their roles in God's salvation history were made explicit (Luke 1:5–38). Luke's narrative seems designed to erase any doubt about how John and Jesus must have viewed each other (one can't imagine that they grew up without ever hearing about each other!), and it clearly highlights Jesus' superior status.

In the Gospel of John, Jesus' baptism does not create any problems, because it is omitted altogether. To be clear, John's ministry of baptism is mentioned, and John testifies to seeing the Spirit descending on Jesus.

But the actual baptism of Jesus is conspicuously absent. Not only that, but John is now *fully* aware of Jesus' heavenly identity. When he sees Jesus, he exclaims, "Here is the Lamb of God who takes away the sin of the world!" Rather than sending two disciples to see if Jesus is really the Messiah, he actually prompts two of his disciples to follow Jesus. Later, John even recognizes that his own ministry has been fulfilled and surpassed by the coming of Jesus. He says of Jesus, "He must increase, but I must decrease" (John 1:28–37).

In short, we can see a clear tendency in the gospels to exaggerate John the Baptist's enthusiasm for Jesus while denying John's spiritual superiority. This tendency only reinforces the fact that Jesus admired John deeply and that he was moved to participate in John's baptism.

Now, why does any of this matter? The answer is that John's whole ministry seems to hinge on the expectation that the end is near. Let's begin with the fact that he is closely associated with Elijah, a famous prophet from the Old Testament. John is described as wearing camel hair and having a leather belt around his waist, which is reminiscent of how the Bible describes Elijah (Mark 1:6).[3] In fact, Jesus later says that John *is* Elijah (Mark 9:13).

In the Old Testament, Elijah is one of the few people who never dies. Instead, he ascends to heaven in a chariot of fire (the story is told in 2 Kings 2:1–12). According to the book of Malachi, God is going to send Elijah shortly before the day of the Lord, which is another way of referring to the day of judgment (see Malachi 3:1; 4:5–6). So when John the Baptist tells his listeners that another, more powerful figure is coming, it strongly suggests that John may see himself in the role of Elijah, and that he is looking ahead to the coming of the Messiah.

Another motif that the Old Testament associates with the coming day of judgment is the outpouring of God's spirit on all people. This event would mark the end of the Jewish exile in foreign nations (Joel 2:28–3:3). John seems to be referring to this when he says that, even though he baptizes people with water, the coming figure will baptize them with the Holy Spirit (Mark 1:8).

In the Q material, John speaks of coming wrath and the need for bearing fruit "worthy of repentance." Additionally, he says that the ax is lying at the root of the tree and that the bad trees will get thrown into the fire (Matthew 3:7–9; Luke 3:7–9). These statements all relate to the imminence of final judgment, and they perfectly complement the message of John found in Mark.

We've already talked about how the Gospel of John tries to deny that Jesus taught that he would return within the lifetime of his disciples, and how it omits Jesus' exorcisms and most of his teachings about the kingdom of God. In fact, many of the elements in Jesus' ministry related to an imminent end are muted or omitted in this gospel. So it should come as no surprise that, whereas the first three gospels closely associate John the Baptist with Elijah, in this gospel John explicitly denies that he is Elijah (John 1:21). This all seems to fit with the idea that the Gospel of John was written in the days when Christians were trying to cope with the fact that Jesus hadn't returned yet. More importantly, it lends credibility to the claim that John the Baptist believed the end to be near.

Now we can see why this matters so much. It's very likely that Jesus admired John the Baptist and participated in his baptism. This means that he must have agreed with the message that John proclaimed. The result is that Jesus is perfectly positioned between a mentor who proclaimed an imminent day of judgment and a movement which proclaimed that the imminent judgment would soon be enacted by Jesus. When we remember that Jesus is overwhelmingly portrayed as someone who preached a similar message, it seems almost certain that he expected the final judgment to occur in the near future, and that he taught his followers accordingly.

The Twelve Disciples

There is one last piece of evidence that we will consider here. One of the most well-known things about Jesus is that he had a group of twelve disciples. Of course, there were other people who followed Jesus (including Mary Magdalene and other women), but early Christian sources agree that there was a group of disciples known as "the Twelve."

All four gospels tell us that Jesus appointed this group of twelve disciples, and the first three gospels agree in calling these men "apostles." The names of the twelve disciples vary somewhat depending on the gospel, and in fact, the Gospel of John does not even tell us all of their names, but merely acknowledges that the group exists (for example, in John 6:70). Paul mentions "the Twelve" without explaining who they are, as if he expects his audience to be familiar with them already (1 Corinthians 15:5). And the book of Revelation also mentions the twelve apostles without naming them (Revelation 21:14).

The varying lists of names in the gospels suggests that membership in the group was not strictly limited to the twelve people that Jesus personally selected. Perhaps it was limited to twelve people *at a time*, but the book of Acts has an early scene where the disciples pick a replacement for Judas Iscariot, who betrayed Jesus and met with an unpleasant end (Acts 1:15–26). It may even be that "the Twelve" continued to function as a recognized group with less than twelve members.

Whatever the case may be, there is a saying found in the Q material where Jesus tells the twelve disciples that they will "sit on twelve thrones, judging the twelve tribes of Israel" (Matthew 19:28; Luke 22:30). This saying has a strong claim to authenticity, since Judas Iscariot is among the twelve when Jesus makes this comment, which makes it seem like Jesus falsely expected Judas to remain loyal to him. At the very least, one questions whether the early Christians would have falsely attributed a comment like this to the man they worshiped as God.

In light of all this evidence, it seems very likely that Jesus really did handpick a special group of twelve disciples. To see why this matters, here is a quick history lesson: Long before the time of Jesus, there were twelve tribes of Israel. According to the Old Testament, each tribe descended from the sons or grandsons of Jacob (who was also called Israel). We often speak about the people of Israel as if they were a single nation, but for a time, the twelve tribes existed as two independent kingdoms. The kingdom in the north, called Israel, was formed by ten of the tribes, while the kingdom in the south, called Judah, was formed by the other two.

Eventually, both of these kingdoms were overtaken by enemy nations. When the northern kingdom of Israel fell to the Assyrians, the people of Israel were exiled from their homeland. As a result, the ten tribes were scattered, and they gradually disappeared as their members were assimilated into other cultures. Thus they are called the Ten Lost Tribes of Israel.

As for the southern kingdom of Judah, its people also went into exile after their kingdom fell to the Babylonians. But after the Babylonians were themselves conquered by the Persians, the people of Judah were allowed to return to their homeland and rebuild their temple in Jerusalem. So the tribes of Judah and Benjamin were not lost as the other ten were (although the tribe of Benjamin was ultimately assimilated into the tribe of Judah).

The loss of the ten tribes was, understandably, a devastating blow to the Jewish people. Naturally, those who hoped that God would someday restore their national independence envisioned that God, in his infinite power and wisdom, could even reverse the seemingly permanent effects of Israel's exile. The Old Testament repeatedly claims that God will eventually regather all the Jewish people from the ends of the earth. Here are just a few examples:

> Even if you are exiled to the ends of the world, from there the Lord your God will gather you, and from there he will take you back. The Lord your God will bring you into the land that your ancestors possessed, and you will possess it; he will make you more prosperous and numerous than your ancestors. (Deuteronomy 30:4–5)

> On that day the Lord will again raise his hand to recover the remnant that is left of his people, from Assyria, from Egypt, from Pathros, from Cush, from Elam, from Shinar, from Hamath, and from the coastlands of the sea. He will raise a signal for the nations and will assemble the outcasts of Israel and gather the dispersed of Judah from the four corners of the earth. (Isaiah 11:11–12)

> At that time I will bring you home, at the time when I gather you; for I will make you renowned and praised among all the peoples of the earth, when I restore your fortunes before your eyes, says the Lord. (Zephaniah 3:20)

As a result, the restoration of the twelve tribes of Israel became a major component of ancient Jewish beliefs about what God would do at the end of the present age. Jesus seems to have shared this expectation, since his belief that the twelve disciples would rule over the twelve tribes assumes that the tribes would be regathered at that point. In fact, there is another saying in Q where Jesus says that "people will come from east and west, from north and south, and take their places at the banquet in the kingdom of God" (Luke 13:29), which fits with this theme as well.

The fact that Jesus felt authorized to call a special group of twelve disciples to follow him is highly significant, especially since he tells them directly that they will rule over the twelve tribes of Israel. Not only does Jesus believe that the twelve tribes will be gathered together, but he seems to think that this will be accomplished through his own ministry. The mere fact that he would even position himself as the leader of the Twelve is highly provocative. Thus, we have another independent line of evidence which strongly suggests that he believed the end to be near.

Did Jesus Change His Mind?

There are a lot of Christians, and a lot of scholars, who deny that Jesus expected the end of the world to arrive in the near future. Yet the evidence we've discussed seems powerful and persuasive. How is it that so many scholars come to a different conclusion?

Everyone seems to agree that Jesus submitted to John's baptism, and there's no getting away from the fact that John proclaimed an imminent final judgment. While one could argue that Jesus differed from John in various respects, the evidence makes it highly unlikely that John's expectation of a quickly-approaching end was a point of disagreement between them. So how can anyone get around this? Some scholars have suggested that, while Jesus embraced John's view of imminent judgment early on, he eventually came to reject it.[4]

As far as I can tell, there are two steps involved in this argument, each of which is problematic. The first step is to assume that a wide body of Jesus' authentic sayings and deeds are incompatible with the idea that he expected the end to arrive while his generation was still alive. For example, Jesus promoted a radical sort of compassion and empathy, and he practiced table fellowship with people who were generally regarded as "sinners" or "unclean." These are often taken to mean that Jesus believed that the kingdom of God was a present reality, and not something that would only arrive in the future.

The main problem with this kind of thinking is that two characteristic features of movements in history that proclaim an imminent cosmic shakeup are that they address the disaffected and promote the removal of social inequalities.[5] It's just a non sequitur to say that Jesus can't have expected an imminent end because he practiced a subversive type of compassion.

It's also a mistake to assume that, if Jesus expected the end to arrive within a generation, then this idea must be reflected in everything he said. For instance, there's a famous passage in the gospels where Jesus teaches that loving God and loving one's neighbor are the two greatest commandments in the Jewish law, and that those who recognize the wisdom in this "are not far from the kingdom of God" (Mark 12:28–34). Some have argued that this is a timeless spiritual message, totally unlike the expectation for an imminent final judgment, and therefore any sayings that speak of imminent judgment must be deemed inauthentic. But this is another non sequitur. Paul affirms the imminence of the end of the world in the same passage where he says that the entire Jewish law is summed up in the commandment to love one's neighbor (Romans 13:9–12). If Paul could hold these ideas together, why assume that Jesus was any different?

The second step of the argument has to do with what Jesus says about John the Baptist in Q: "Truly I tell you, among those born of women no one is greater than John, yet the least in the kingdom of God is greater than he" (Matthew 11:11; Luke 7:28). A version of this saying also appears in the Gospel of Thomas (verse 46). Since the two halves of this statement seem to conflict with each other, some scholars take this as evidence that Jesus changed his mind about John's message. The first half is what Jesus originally thought, and the second half is his revised view.

Unfortunately, the logic here is quite flimsy. We're just not in any position to study the development of Jesus' thinking over time, since he didn't leave us with any writings of his own. Even if the two statements really do contradict each other, can we be sure that it wasn't Jesus' followers who added the second clause?

To make matters worse, the whole motivation for distancing Jesus from the idea of an imminent final judgment is to avoid associating him with unfulfilled time-sensitive predictions, as well as with a number of unpleasant sayings concerning hell and divine wrath. Yet once we've admitted that Jesus was, at any point in his ministry, on board with these ideas, the game is up. For in that case, we no longer have any firm basis for denying that the problematic teachings go back to Jesus, since it's perfectly reasonable to think that they originated with the "earlier" Jesus.

We should also notice a glaring inconsistency in how certain scholars approach the gospel material. There is wide agreement on the fact that John the Baptist proclaimed an imminent final judgment. Yet we have far more sayings material for Jesus, from a wider variety of sources, than we do for John. In Jesus' case we have even more evidence, since we know that he selected twelve disciples (which has obvious relevant significance to Jewish expectations about what God would do at the end of the present age), and the movement he started insisted that the end would arrive quickly. So why is the gospel material sufficient for saying that John proclaimed an imminent final judgment, but not for saying the same thing about Jesus? It doesn't really make sense.

Final Thoughts

Those who doubt that Jesus predicted an imminent final judgment have sometimes asked how Christianity could have spread so successfully if its founder made such a blatantly false claim. But notice that this question would persist even if Jesus didn't believe in the imminent end of the world. After all, regardless of what Jesus thought, his followers certainly claimed that the end was near, and they portrayed Jesus as teaching this too. Yet somehow Christianity succeeded in spite of this. So even though it's an interesting question as to how Christianity thrived in spite of an obviously false teaching from its founder, that alone is not a good enough reason to deny that the teaching originates with Jesus.

In short, there is compelling evidence that Jesus proclaimed an imminent final judgment to his followers. Whether he believed this consistently throughout his ministry is not as important to me, although I see no good reason to doubt it. Since the final judgment never took place, it follows that Jesus' ministry was built on a major false claim about God. This strikes me as a powerful reason to deny his spiritual authority. Therefore, we have strong grounds for denying that Jesus is God.

Chapter 5
Liars and Lunatics

In the first chapter, I gave a positive assessment of certain aspects of Jesus' vision of God. However, Christian apologists frequently argue that it doesn't make sense to think highly of Jesus' teachings unless you worship him. Of course, I wouldn't say that I think highly of *all* of Jesus' teachings—I certainly am not impressed with his false predictions about the imminent final judgment—but let's put that aside for now.

The argument we are considering claims that, if Jesus falsely claimed to be God, then those who admire him seem to face a rather troubling dilemma. Either he was intentionally lying, which makes him profoundly evil and manipulative, or he thought he was telling the truth, in which case he must have been completely insane. Each of these alternatives would make Jesus a very unsettling figure.

Therefore, if we really think that Jesus was a legitimately good person of sound mind, then logically (so the argument goes) we are obligated to affirm his divinity. And, since I have argued that Jesus was not God, in light of his false teachings, I seem to be in the awkward position of having to deny that Jesus was a good person with at least some good ideas.

This is sometimes called the "lunatic, liar, or Lord" argument, and it was famously defended by C. S. Lewis in his book *Mere Christianity:*

> A man who was merely a man and said the sort of things
> Jesus said would not be a great moral teacher. He would

either be a lunatic—on a level with the man who says he
is a poached egg—or else he would be the Devil of Hell.
You must make your choice. Either this man was, and is,
the Son of God: or else a madman or something worse.
. . . Now it seems to me obvious that He was neither a
lunatic nor a fiend: and consequently, however strange or
terrifying or unlikely it may seem, I have to accept the view
that He was and is God.[1]

Many critics of this argument have complained that it fails to consider
all of the logical alternatives. They point out that the stories in the gospels
could be legends, or that Jesus may have claimed to be an exalted human
figure without also claiming to be divine. But notice, these are not really
objections to the dilemma itself. Rather, they are objections to the idea
that Jesus claimed to be God. The question is, *if Jesus claimed to be God*,
what should we make of him?

One might speculate that Jesus was joking, but this only works if you
completely ignore the gospels. And even if a person jokingly claims to be
God, they're not *really* claiming to be God, and that is obviously what
the argument is getting at. Another possibility that I've heard is that
perhaps Jesus was simply mistaken, but this seems a bit silly once you
stop to think about it. Can a person of sound mind accidentally mistake
themselves for the creator of the universe? Somehow I doubt it.

However, there is some potential ambiguity in the phrase "claims to
be God." What kind of God are we talking about? In a setting where
people believe that every person has an inner divine nature, claiming to
be God could mean something entirely different from what it would
mean inside a conservative Baptist church on a Sunday morning. Lewis
himself recognized this possible ambiguity and made it clear that he was

talking about the God of Israel: "God, in their language, meant the Being outside the world, who had made it and was infinitely different from anything else."[2] For someone to claim in all seriousness to be this kind of God would certainly be astounding. Unless they were telling the truth, we would have to think that they were either the victim of a terrible delusion or a depraved opportunist.

It seems very unlikely to me that Jesus would intentionally try to deceive his followers. Liars don't usually stick to their guns to the point of being crucified. Does this mean that, if we have good reason to deny Jesus' divinity, we must conclude that he is on the same level as a man who thinks he's a poached egg? Did a poached egg man ever go around preaching a message of compassion in light of a coming egg apocalypse? (If so, let's hope that the apocalypse will be over easy.)

Perhaps it would be easier to deny that Jesus ever claimed to be God, but then we have to contend with the gospels. In spite of all their false-hoods and exaggerations, the gospels say a lot of things about Jesus that are actually true. So we are left with two big questions to tackle. First, did Jesus really claim to be God? And second, are we really forced to choose between worshiping him or dismissing him as a lunatic?

Jesus' Divinity in the Gospels

The Gospel of John tells us, in no uncertain terms, that Jesus is God. In its famous prologue, it says that Jesus existed with God the Father prior to becoming human, and that he played a direct role in the creation of the world (John 1:1–14). In keeping with this idea, the author of John depicts Jesus as openly claiming to be God on multiple occasions. At one point Jesus says, "The Father and I are one" (John 10:30). Elsewhere he declares, "Very truly, I tell you, before Abraham was, I am" (John 8:58).

This is an explicit claim to divinity, since the sacred name of Israel's God, Yahweh, is based on how God reveals himself to Moses as "I am" in the book of Exodus (see Exodus 3:13–15).

However, we already know that the portrait of Jesus found in the Gospel of John is heavily embellished, and in many ways it seems to revise Jesus' story in order to downplay his proclamation of an imminent end, which is strongly attested in the other three gospels. It would therefore be supremely unwise to treat John's portrayal of Jesus as historical fact. This is why Christian scholars who defend Jesus' claims to divinity tend to focus on the other three gospels.

Now, the authors of the first three gospels also viewed Jesus as divine. I am not sure if they would have agreed with John's portrayal of Jesus as existing prior to his birth, but I don't think it's implausible. Christians were already affirming the pre-existence of Jesus by the middle of the first century, before any of the gospels were written. This is clearest in a passage from Paul's letter to the Philippians, where Jesus is depicted as having "the form of God" before appearing as a human (Philippians 2:6–11). The exact meaning of this passage is debated, especially when it comes to the phrase "the form of God," but the passage certainly affirms Jesus' pre-existence.

In any case, the first three gospels unquestionably portray Jesus as divine. In Matthew and Luke, God is literally his father, since he is the one who impregnated Jesus' mother. Then, at the end of Matthew, Jesus commands his disciples to baptize in "the name of the Father and of the Son and of the Holy Spirit" (Matthew 28:19), which seems to put Jesus, the Father, and the Holy Spirit on the same level, especially since they apparently share a name.

Furthermore, the first three gospels portray Jesus as having power over nature in a way that seems designed to invite comparison with God's power over nature in the Old Testament. For instance, when Jesus and his disciples are caught in a bad storm while out in a boat, he calms the storm by verbally rebuking it. As a result, the disciples rightly ask, "Who then is this, that even the wind and the sea obey him?" (Mark 4:41).[3]

The real question is whether we should trust these depictions of Jesus, given their miraculous content. I don't mean that miracles are impossible, or that rational people can't believe in them. But since the gospels were written by men who worshiped Jesus and who weren't afraid to embellish or exaggerate the truth, it would be foolish to accept their testimony about Jesus' amazing powers without further question. At the very least, we should remain skeptical unless we have a compelling reason to think otherwise. I will return to this topic in the next chapter, since there is much more that needs to be said about it.

So, what did Jesus actually claim for himself? Did he claim to be God? Did he say anything that would give people the impression that he was a divine figure?

Messiah and Son of God

Here I want to breeze past a couple of important debates, simply because I have no quarrel with Christian apologists on these fronts. I am personally convinced that Jesus intentionally spoke and acted in ways that gave people the impression that he was the Messiah.

One important piece of evidence here (though by no means the only one) is the fact that Jesus was crucified under the charge of claiming to be "the King of the Jews" (Mark 15:26). This detail is not likely to be a Christian invention, since "King of the Jews" was not a Christian title for Jesus, and it helps make sense of why Jesus would have been executed by the Roman state as opposed to just being whipped, imprisoned, or ignored completely. Contrary to what many people seem to think, if Jesus was only telling people to love each other, the empire wouldn't have killed him. Whatever Jesus said or did, it gave the Roman governor the impression that he saw himself as a rival king, and there's no evidence that Jesus denied this charge.

There are also a number of sayings which support the idea that Jesus claimed to be the Son of God. Significantly, we have the parable of the wicked tenants, which is independently attested by the Gospel of Mark (Mark 12:1–12) and the Gospel of Thomas (Thomas 65). Remember that in this parable, Jesus depicts himself as the son of a vineyard owner who is sent to the tenants in one final attempt to collect payment from them before the owner finally destroys them. Thus, Jesus sees himself both as God's Son and as God's final messenger to a wicked generation. This parable offers a great example of how hard it is to separate Jesus' claim that the end is near from his highly exalted view of himself.

Additionally, we must remember that Jesus had a specially designated group of twelve disciples. We have seen that this group was almost certainly meant to represent the scattered tribes of Israel, whom Jesus expected to be gathered together in the near future as part of God's plan to put an end to the present age of suffering. But notice that Jesus does not position himself as one of the twelve. Rather, he is their leader. By this act alone, he seems to envision himself as the one who would lead God's people into the new, eternal age.

Of course, claiming to be the Messiah does not necessarily imply a claim to divinity, since the Messiah was widely expected to be a human figure who would rule over the people of Israel. Nor does claiming to be the Son of God, for that matter, since this could just be another way of claiming to be the Messiah. We noted earlier that, in the Old Testament, the king of Israel could be called the son of God, even the "begotten" son of God, but this was a symbolic claim about his uniquely authoritative status. So even though Jesus unquestionably makes big claims about his authority, this does not automatically suggest a divine self-conception.

To illustrate my point, consider Jesus' response when the chief priests ask him directly about his authority. Instead of answering their question, he asks them where they think John the Baptist's authority came from (John, by this point, had already been killed). The chief priests refuse to answer because (according to the story) any answer they give will make them look bad. Jesus likewise refuses to comment on his own authority (Mark 11:27–33). Nevertheless, it is clear that Jesus regards both himself and John as having been divinely authorized to carry out their respective ministries. Yet Jesus certainly didn't regard John as a divine being worthy of worship. So if he also saw himself as an authoritative figure, it does not necessarily mean that he claimed to be God.

Son of Man

But now things become more complicated. Throughout the gospels, Jesus often refers to himself as the Son of Man. Sometimes this involves a direct reference to the "Son of Man" prophecy from Daniel, as when Jesus talks about the Son of Man coming with the clouds of heaven. Apologists frequently claim that, since Daniel's Son of Man is a highly exalted figure who approaches God's throne and is given everlasting dominion over all creation, he is plainly meant to be a divine figure. Therefore, by calling himself the Son of Man, Jesus is claiming to be divine—at least, that's the argument.[4] But does it hold up?

In the original passage, Daniel's words about the Son of Man follow a vision of four terrible beasts coming out of the sea. The beasts are defeated just before the Son of Man appears and receives his authority from God. A heavenly interpreter then explains the meaning of both the beasts and the Son of Man: "As for these four great beasts, four kings shall arise out of the earth. But the holy ones of the Most High shall receive the kingdom and possess the kingdom forever—forever and ever" (Daniel 7:17–18). In other words, just as the beasts are meant to symbolize four kings, the Son of Man is meant to symbolize the holy ones of God, who will receive the kingdom forever. Debate centers on whether the "holy ones" are supposed to be angels or humans, but it's notable that the Son of Man is never identified as God.

In line with many of his contemporaries, Jesus viewed the Son of Man as a cosmic being who would someday appear from heaven and judge the world, but this does not necessarily mean that he also expected the Son of Man to be a divine figure worthy of worship. Highly exalted? Yes, absolutely. On an equal footing with God? Possible, but far from certain.

Defenders of Jesus' divine claims often appeal to Mark's account of Jesus' hearing before the Judean council after his arrest. The high priest asks Jesus directly, "Are you the Messiah, the Son of the Blessed One?" In response Jesus says, "I am, and 'you will see the Son of Man seated at the right hand of the Power' and 'coming on the clouds of heaven'" (Mark 14:61–62). Jesus is immediately condemned for blasphemy. The charge of blasphemy would not necessarily stem from claiming to be the Messiah. Rather, it seems to be directed at Jesus' claim that he will be seated at God's right hand, thus sharing God's authority.

However, the historical accuracy of this scene is often doubted by scholars. As far as we know, the disciples had already deserted Jesus when he was arrested. Peter was still around, but he was out in the courtyard. Was anybody else transcribing the trial? Was the information reliably preserved for Christian writers forty years later? It seems possible, but all we have is the word of Mark, which is insufficient for establishing a firm conclusion about what really happened.

Even if we can't be sure of what Jesus said to the Judean council, it seems quite likely that he spoke about the Son of Man's imminent appearance. This raises another interesting question: was Jesus talking about himself, or someone else?

Some scholars have argued that Jesus expected the arrival of a different cosmic figure, and that this is who he was talking about when he said that the Son of Man would soon appear to gather God's people and carry out the final judgment.[5] Some of Jesus' sayings are surprisingly easy to read in this fashion (for example, Mark 8:38). Even though Christian apologists sometimes balk at the idea that Jesus could have expected there to be another central figure on God's stage besides himself, the idea is not that far-fetched, since we know from the Dead Sea Scrolls that some members of the Jewish community were waiting for two Messiahs.[6]

Still, the third-person language is not decisive. If Jesus talked about himself as the Son of God, then he seems to have used third-person language to refer to himself in other contexts (for instance, in Matthew 11:27). It seems likely to me that Jesus expected to be the one who would enact God's judgment, so I am less inclined to think that he was waiting for a different figure to appear, although I remain open to the possibility.

Delusions of Grandeur

Suppose we conclude that Jesus really did claim to be authorized by God to speak and act on his behalf, and that he expected to be at the center of the "end of the world" drama. This may not get us all the way to saying that "Jesus claimed to be God," but it is still a pretty highly exalted view of himself. Additionally, we've already seen that his ministry was based on a major false claim about what God was going to do in the near future. This all certainly gives the impression that Jesus was delusional to some degree. Does this mean that he was a lunatic?

I find the word "lunatic" and its synonyms to be supremely unhelpful in this context, because they don't allow us to deal with the complexity of what it means to say that someone is mentally unhealthy. We must also remember that the ministry of Jesus was not the only case from this general time period in which a Jewish movement centered around a figure making exalted claims for himself. Other similar movements gained enough momentum to invite Roman intervention.[7]

Perhaps we would say that the men who organized these movements had delusions of grandeur, but they did not exist in a vacuum. The Jewish people had a long and difficult history with their non-Jewish rulers, and they often tried to make sense of their experiences within the framework provided by a rich, deeply complicated biblical tradition. How could we possibly understand, with our limited evidence, what was going through their heads?

Jesus was not engaging in detached theological reflection. He was a member of the lower-class living in the shadow of the Roman empire who became fully convinced that God was about to fulfill his promises to deliver his people from their suffering. Somehow, he also became convinced that he himself had a central role to play in that story. His message resonated well enough with others that he was able to lead a group of disciples, cause a disturbance in the Jewish temple at the time of Passover, and get himself in trouble with the Roman governor in Judea.

If, in light of all this, Jesus came to see himself in a highly exalted role, would that call his sanity into question? I think he must have been delusional to some extent, but I don't know the exact context or manner in which his thought developed, and I don't think it's possible to diagnose someone's mental health based on the limited evidence we can pull from sacred biographies that are almost two thousand years old.

In the end, I don't claim to know exactly what Jesus' deal was. I think he envisioned himself doing great things. I also think he was wrong in regard to God's plan for history and his own role in that plan, and wrong on a number of other issues too. However, to whatever extent the gospels do reflect his teachings accurately, he seems to have hit upon certain ideas about God that have had great staying power.

I don't see any reason to see this as historically implausible, since people with mental health issues are not necessarily incapable of being insightful. At least, there is no good reason to paint with such a broad brush. So, contrary to what many Christian apologists have claimed, it seems possible to affirm Jesus' sincerity and deny his divinity without resorting to simplistic, over-the-top labels for his mental health. To say it more clearly, one does not need to worship Jesus simply to avoid having to call him a lunatic.

Chapter 6

Miracles

It seems that most scholars are willing to regard Jesus as a healer. I'm not sure how many would say that his healings were actual miracles, but the widespread acknowledgement of Jesus' status as a healer is based on the fact that his abilities are attested in all of the gospel sources, including the earliest ones. Not only that, but certain sayings which have a fair claim to authenticity indicate that Jesus saw himself as a miracle worker (see Matthew 11:4-5; Luke 11:20). The topic of miracles thus demands careful attention.

The Philosophical Problem of Miracles

It's impossible to talk about miracles without thinking of David Hume's famous essay on the topic. "But it is a miracle, that a dead man should come to life," Hume writes, "because that has never been observed, in any age or country. There must, therefore, be a uniform experience against every miraculous event, otherwise the event would not merit that appellation."[1] Of course, to say that no miracle has ever been observed, and that there is a *uniform experience* against such a thing happening, is to assume from the outset that no miracle story is true. If any miracle has ever been observed by any person on any occasion, then Hume is wrong to say that there's a uniform experience against miracles. So how can we be sure that no miracle has ever been observed?

Hume attempts to support his idea of a uniform experience against miracles by drawing generalizations about the kinds of people who report on miracles. But this is not a very compelling strategy, since it's one thing to say that most people who report on miracles are wrong, and an entirely different thing to say that all of them have always been wrong, even in cases that we've never personally considered. If we're going to treat the uniform experience against miracles as an established fact, then we need something more than a generalization based on stereotypes. That's not how rational inquiry is supposed to work.

One could try to simplify things by defining miracles in such a way that they are impossible by definition, but any such definition can always be challenged by those who believe in miracles. For instance, many philosophers (Hume included) have defined miracles as "violations of the laws of nature." If we take the laws of nature to be "exceptionless regularities," then a miracle would be an exception to an exceptionless regularity, which is a logical contradiction.

However, believers in miracles do not deny that the universe operates by fixed natural laws. They simply think that certain events are caused by powers that are not part of the natural system. If some supernatural entity should interfere with the system, that does not mean that the system was not operating by laws, or that the laws won't continue to operate moving forward. It means, rather, that at a certain point in space and time, something happened that could not possibly have happened by natural causes. To say that this sort of thing is impossible, by definition, is a mere assertion. What we need is an argument. We cannot settle the debate just by defining controversial terms to our liking.

Skeptics of miracles could say that, even if we don't have proof that there is a uniform experience against miracles, it at least seems likely that there must be such a uniform experience. Yet if we try to use that uniform experience as an argument against the rationality of believing in any miracle, we'll simply end up reasoning in a circle: *I've never been convinced by any miracle claim that I've heard, therefore no miracle has ever been observed, and since no miracle has ever been observed, I cannot be convinced by any miracle claim.*

Skeptical discourse about miracles doesn't seem to have advanced much since Hume's time. For example, Bart Ehrman, a world-class New Testament scholar, has often stated words to the effect that "historians can only establish what probably happened, and miracles by their definition are the least probable occurrences."[2] One is tempted to ask, "By whose definition?" The problem here is that probabilities are influenced by things we already know and by specific evidence related to the case at hand. Unless our background knowledge includes a successful argument against the likelihood of any miracles, it is question-begging to assume, without further discussion (and prior to considering any evidence), that miracles are always improbable.

Skeptics frequently declare that any non-miraculous explanation, no matter how outlandish, will always be more probable than a miracle. Ehrman says (and watch him subtly change his definition here), "From a purely historical point of view, a highly unlikely event is far more probable than a virtually impossible one."[3] But again, why should we just assume that miracles are "virtually impossible"? Why are all non-miraculous explanations, no matter how bizarre, somehow more intrinsically probable than a miracle hypothesis formed in direct response to the relevant evidence?

Suppose that after his death, Jesus' body was stolen from its resting place by aliens, and then an alien pretended to be him to convince people that he was raised back to life. Technically, this would not be a miracle, since if aliens exist, they exist in our universe and are subject to the same physical laws. Even so, the alien hypothesis is ridiculous, and any scholar who offers it as an actual theory is probably being paid by the History Channel. So how do we know, without even looking at any evidence, that this event is somehow more likely than Jesus being raised back to life by a divine power?

A believer could agree that miracles are improbable in the sense of being far less frequent than non-miraculous occurrences, but this is not the same thing as measuring the probability that a miracle has happened on any specific occasion, which would require an evaluation of the evidence related to that particular case. Furthermore, if you have a divine agent in the mix whose intentions remain hidden from us and which can freely choose (as often or as sparingly as it wants) to interfere with the ordinary course of events in the world, we have no way of knowing in advance that it will never do such a thing.

Thus, it seems to be more of a philosophical question about the kind of world we live in, and about whether there is a divine reality that can cause miracles in the first place. To ignore this question would be to decide the outcome of the discussion in advance, as a matter of pure bias. Again, this is not how rational inquiry is supposed to proceed.

Many skeptics of miracles appeal to a philosophy called *naturalism*, which holds that the universe is a closed system of physical, material, or natural causes and their effects. Since it is a closed system, there is no room for supernatural causes. Now people have offered many arguments in favor of naturalism, and I don't intend to explore that issue here. Rather, my point is that we cannot discount miracles on principle by appealing to naturalism as if it were a self-evident truth. Why not? Because this would be the same thing as asserting that there is a uniform experience against miracles. If any miracle has ever happened, naturalism is false. Those of us who remain skeptical of naturalism will not be much impressed by the mere assertion that miracles have never been observed.

Miracles as Evidence for Religious Claims

It might seem odd to have spent so much time in a book like this criticizing skeptical arguments against miracles, but it was a necessary ground-clearing exercise. If I thought that miracles were impossible, or that they were always improbable by definition, then there would be little point in everything else I've talked about so far. I could simply argue that Jesus wasn't God because that would be a miracle. But since I do not see any good reason to accept the claims of naturalism, and since the evidence has led me to remain firmly in the theist camp, I have no argument to make against miracles in general.

Theologians usually distinguish between miracles and other kinds of divine providence. In theory, God could arrange the universe in such a way that, at a specific point in time, someone's prayer will be answered by an event that happens as part of the ordinary course of events. By contrast, a miracle is not part of the ordinary course of events. It is something that requires the intervention of a supernatural power.

What this means is that if an unexpected rainstorm suddenly provides life-saving water to someone on the brink of death, or if a stranger pays your hospital bill, these are not necessarily miracles. However, if a truly dead person returns to life after three days, that's certainly a miracle. In the absence of any supernatural interference, dead people have this pesky habit of staying dead.

Apologists often appeal to miracles as evidence for the truth of their religious beliefs. However, there are lots of stories involving miraculous events that don't seem to have anything to do with religious ideas. I know a family who can tell you some of the most interesting stories you've ever heard: a child being dragged by an invisible force out of the way of a falling TV; a large, precarious tree branch being lifted up into the air by an unseen force and placed safely on the ground; and lots of other good ones (along with a few terrifying ones). Do I believe all their stories? Not really. But if I did, what would it prove? I suppose it would suggest that there are supernatural forces, and sometimes these forces help people, even though most of the time they don't.

Of course, some miracle stories do seem to have religious significance. For example, there's a preacher who claims that God commanded him audibly to write a book about how being poor is a sin.[4] If such a thing were true, it would be hugely significant, but I don't feel very optimistic about it. Even if this event happened in a room full of witnesses who all claimed to have heard the same voice coming out of the sky, lots of people, including lots of Christians, would still probably doubt that it proved anything about God's attitude toward poverty, not because there's a way to disprove the miracle, but because the pastor's theology doesn't square with his alleged commitment to Jesus, and in any case, it's a horrible theology to begin with.

This, I think, is the real problem with using miracles as evidence for one's religious beliefs. If your theology doesn't make sense to me, or if it strikes me as evil, I'm not going to come around to it even in the face of apparently strong evidence for a miracle. Still, this doesn't seem like a good enough reason to reject all miracle stories as fabrications.

Whatever personal skepticism I have toward miracles is influenced more by the question of why God would miraculously intervene on some occasions, but not others. Why would God sometimes cure people of cancer but allow millions of Jewish children to suffer brutal deaths during the Holocaust? Why would God sometimes mend broken bones in an instant while doing nothing to prevent the genocide in Gaza? I can't make sense of it, so I find it very difficult to believe. But for whatever it's worth I remain open-minded about miracles.

Christian apologists often claim that miracles provide an overwhelming confirmation of Christianity's truth. One miracle in particular is usually thought to provide strong evidential support: the resurrection of Jesus. For this reason, the debate over Christianity's truth often centers on the question of whether or not Jesus actually rose from the dead. However, before we talk about the resurrection, it's worth exploring certain general difficulties that come up in regard to Jesus' miracles.

The Miracles of Jesus

Some of Jesus' contemporaries reportedly attributed his powers to evil spirits (Mark 3:22). If this is true, it may be that Jesus' abilities were hard to deny and had to be explained away somehow. Alternatively, these criticisms may simply reflect the exasperation that some of his critics felt at his overwhelming popularity as a miracle worker. In other words, accusations of being in cahoots with the Devil might not have come from people who actually witnessed Jesus' ministry firsthand, but from people who only heard stories about him.

If Jesus was anywhere near as popular as the gospels make him out to be, then it is likely that stories about him were already being embellished while he was still alive, especially in a culture where information like this was spread primarily by word of mouth. Sometimes apologists claim that this sort of early legendary development would have been impossible because, if a false story about Jesus was told, somebody would have spoken up and challenged or corrected it. This assumes, among other things, that eyewitnesses were always present when stories about Jesus were told. But we have no way to determine just how many individual people played a hand in passing along the stories and traditions contained in the gospels, or how many of them had actually seen Jesus for themselves.

I don't want to seem dismissive of scholarship concerning the nature of oral traditions in a society like the one Jesus lived in. There is no doubt that, in an oral culture, a story could take on a fixed form and then be repeated many times without losing its basic structure. Joke-telling provides a helpful analogy because it is one way that, even today, we continue to pass on oral traditions in a relatively fixed form. This is why I'm still able to remember jokes that my friends told me when I was in elementary school, even though I never wrote them down. The form of a joke is what makes it memorable and easy to share with other people. We may not remember every detail from the version that was shared with us, but as long as we get the setup and the punchline right, the joke will still work.

Yet this certainly doesn't imply the basic reliability of stories passed along in this fashion. There have always been, and always will be, people who purposely change or make up stories. And some people, as we all know, are really bad at telling jokes. It's reasonable to think that, as stories about Jesus were passed along by word of mouth, elements were changed, distorted, omitted, and invented. Given what we know about the nature of human memory, even eyewitnesses with a commitment to truth could have gotten key details wrong.[5] I remember once hearing a friend recount an event as if he were present for it, only for him to be reminded that, when the event happened, he was actually in a different country. He was understandably embarrassed, and the rest of us were perplexed. Human memory is wild and notoriously unreliable.[6]

Again, it seems likely that communities were probably already sharing stories about Jesus before he died. Who would have been providing oversight to make sure that nobody distorted the truth? And what if different communities told different stories? Would one community be able to "correct" another community? What if two people in the same community simply agreed to disagree? We already know, beyond any reasonable doubt, that the gospels contain many false historical claims. Thus, regardless of what we think about the integrity of oral traditions, and whether we like it or not, false stories about Jesus made their way past the guardians of the tradition.

In fact, it is likely that legends about Jesus took root at an early stage. For instance, if we look at Q, which is thought by many scholars to be earlier than the Gospel of Mark, we find the story of Jesus' temptation by Satan in the wilderness (Matthew 4:1–11; Luke 4:1–13). This story reads almost like a fable: Jesus versus the Devil; three temptations; seeing all the kingdoms of the world "in an instant" or from "a very high mountain." I remember once hearing a Christian defend this last detail by saying that the Devil must have shown Jesus all the kingdoms in something like a PowerPoint presentation. One thinks it might just be easier to treat the story as a legend. Also, if my overall argument in *Politely Rejecting the Bible* is correct and the Bible is not a divine product, then the fact that one of the characters in this story is Satan, a mythic figure from the Old Testament, is a clear indicator that this event did not really happen as narrated.[7]

Given the presence of false and embellished material in the gospels, it's reasonable to suspect that Jesus' abilities were greatly exaggerated. And there are a few intriguing details in the gospels—suggestive, but not conclusive—which lend further support to this claim.

The most interesting one, in my opinion, concerns the fact that Jesus was well known as an exorcist, and there are many stories in the gospels where he releases people from the control of "unclean spirits." Consid-

er, then, Jesus' strange comments in Q concerning unclean spirits that
return after leaving a person:

> When the unclean spirit has gone out of a person, it wan-
> ders through waterless regions looking for a resting place,
> but not finding any it says, "I will return to my house
> from which I came." When it returns, it finds it swept and
> put in order. Then it goes and brings seven other spirits
> more evil than itself, and they enter and live there; and
> the last state of that person is worse than the first. (Luke
> 11:24–26; see also Matthew 12:43–45)

In both Matthew and Luke, this teaching occurs in a wider context
where Jesus is defending the legitimacy of his exorcisms, since some of
his critics accuse him of being in league with the Devil. In response, Jesus
is offering an explanation for why an unclean spirit would return to a
person after being driven away from them.

It seems unlikely that Jesus would have talked about this if he didn't
know of at least one case where an unclean spirit was apparently cast out
of a person but didn't stay out. Some scholars have suggested that Jesus
may be referring to a situation that he faced in his own ministry.[8] After
all, his explanation about the unclean spirit returning does not involve
any sort of criticism of the exorcist.

In other words, Jesus is not saying, "Sometimes the spirit returns,
bringing more spirits with it, because it was not properly cast out."
Instead, he's offering an explanation that has nothing to do with the
exorcist. Why does the evil spirit come back? Because it couldn't find any
other place to rest. Such an explanation could, if needed, get an exorcist
off the hook for a botched job. Again, this is not conclusive proof of

anything, and it certainly doesn't require us to believe in the existence of unclean spirits, but it may provide some evidence that Jesus' exorcisms were not always deemed to be successful.

In light of what I've discussed so far, it's no surprise that I'm somewhat skeptical of Jesus' miraculous abilities. Still, I don't feel any need to insist that miracles could never have happened in the context of Jesus' ministry. There are lots of interesting reports from a variety of contexts where people witnessed seemingly miraculous events that can't just be written off as delusions or hallucinations.[9] Since I have no idea what to make of these stories, I am unwilling to offer any definitive comments in regard to Jesus. However, before ending this discussion, there is an interesting theological paradox concerning Jesus' miracles that we must consider.

The Theological Problem of Miracles

It seems fair to say that Jesus can't be God unless miracles are possible. But within a traditional Christian framework, God is not the only being that can cause miracles. Jesus teaches that some evil people who do not belong in his kingdom will still be able to cast out demons, perform deeds of power, and prophesy in his name (Matthew 7:21–23). He also gives warnings about the future appearance of false prophets who will perform great wonders in an attempt to deceive God's people (Matthew 24:24–25).

According to the Bible, Satan's power is quite impressive. In the story of Job, Satan sends fire from heaven to destroy people (Job 1:12–16), which is reminiscent of a similar miracle performed by one of God's legitimate prophets (see 1 Kings 18:38–39). In the book of Revelation, Satan is depicted as a terrible dragon who is able to share his power with another figure, depicted as a beast. As a result, the beast can recover from a mortal wound and persecute the people of God (Revelation 13:1–15).

Christians do not always agree that whatever the Bible says is true, and they don't usually interpret books like Job or Revelation in a strict literal sense. However, since these ideas were part of Jesus' religious context, and since Jesus spoke of false prophets performing miracles in his name, we can modify our earlier statement: Jesus cannot be God unless miracles are possible, and this must include the possibility of Satanic miracles. An openness to Jesus requires an openness to the idea that not all miracles are from God.

As I mentioned earlier, Christian apologists often attempt to demonstrate the truth of Jesus' message in light of the evidence for his miracles. But if Satanic miracles can occur, then there's no way for us to determine the origin of anyone's miracles just by studying the historical evidence. All the historical evidence can do, perhaps, is tell us whether the event happened. A sincere openness to Jesus thus makes it impossible to determine the truth of his claims by appealing to the evidence of his miracles.

When discussing the resurrection of Jesus, Christian apologetics resources often claim that the meaning of any miracle must be determined by its religious context. Yet Jesus' religious context allows for Satanic miracles and false prophets. Even if a miracle was supported by tremendous evidence and came with the message, "I am God and I did this," we still would not know if the message was trustworthy, because the whole point of a Satanic miracle is to deceive. An evil supernatural agent is probably not going to perform a miracle and then say, "I did this miracle, and I am evil and untrustworthy." An evil being may perform miracles in a religiously significant context precisely because it wishes to deceive people. Yet if we deny that this kind of deception is a real possibility, then we must deny the credibility of Jesus' teachings.

Conservative theologians have sometimes tried to set arbitrary limits on what demonic beings can and can't do, but the level of power which the Bible grants to Satan (such as healing someone from a mortal wound) suggests that he could easily create the illusion of a death and resurrection. Historical evidence alone wouldn't be able to determine the difference between a divine miracle and a Satanic counterfeit.

To make matters even more complicated, the Bible also allows for the possibility that God himself will send false prophets who can successfully predict omens and portents while calling on people to worship false gods. Why on earth would God do such a thing? In order to test his people, to see if they will remain loyal to him (Deuteronomy 13:1–3). This is strange for a number of reasons, not least because it conflicts with the idea that a prophet's legitimacy can be identified based on the success of his predictions. The Bible presents Moses as affirming both ideas, even though they can't really be reconciled. In any case, the Old Testament clearly teaches that God can send false prophets who can make successful predictions.

Some apologists say that Jesus can't be a false prophet because he didn't encourage people to worship any other god besides Yahweh. But this really begs the question, doesn't it? After all, many Jewish people would say that it's a grave error to worship any human being as God, and doesn't the Christian believe that Jesus received worship from his followers? It's very convenient to say, "Yes, but Jesus is the same God as Yahweh," but the only people who actually think this way are Jesus' followers. From an outsider perspective, isn't that just the sort of thing you'd expect a false teacher to say?

If Christians are willing to put their faith in a successful miracle worker without worrying about where his power comes from, all it really means is that they don't take the threat of spiritual deception as seriously as Jesus teaches them to. But once we take Jesus on his own terms, in his own religious context, we have no choice but to ask how we can tell if his miracles are authentic. Since historical evidence can't answer that question for us, we have no way to know if Jesus is telling the truth even if he performs amazing miracles.

The only way out of this paradox is either to reject Jesus' message or to accept his message on something other than evidential grounds. And since we already know that his message is built on a false proclamation, the first option seems far more reasonable to me.

Chapter 7

The Resurrection

One of the most popular arguments for Jesus' divinity is the historical argument for his resurrection. Of course, being brought back to life after dying does not prove that someone is divine, but if Jesus made exalted claims about himself, his resurrection would seem to be his ultimate vindication. The argument for Jesus' resurrection has received sophisticated and highly detailed defenses from a number of Christian scholars. In order to make sense of the issue, I will lay out the historical evidence as best I can.

Relevant Historical Sources

A number of early Christian sources, including Paul's letters, preserve multiple confessional formulas about the resurrection that probably originated in the context of early Christian worship. Perhaps the most significant early tradition is one we've already talked about: Paul's creedal formula containing an affirmation of Jesus' death, burial, and resurrection as well as a list of witnesses to whom Jesus appeared (1 Corinthians 15:3–8).

It's not clear exactly how much Paul adds to the list of witnesses, but the original tradition very likely dates back to the earliest days of the church.[1] This passage provides us with our only early record of Jesus' postmortem appearances to his brother James and to a crowd of more than five hundred people at once.

Then we have the narratives at the end of each gospel. The earliest account comes from the Gospel of Mark. It's important to note that there are several "endings" to Mark which are preserved in the ancient manuscripts, including the passage which appears as Mark 16:9–20 in most English Bibles, but these endings were all added to the text by later writers or copyists. None of them are authentic. Even conservative Christian Bible translations usually indicate that the last chapter of Mark ends with verse 8.

Mark's resurrection narrative is thus quite simple: Early on the Sunday morning following Jesus' death, a group of women, including Mary Magdalene, go to his tomb to anoint his body with spices. When they arrive, the tomb is unsealed and the body is missing. A young man, presumably an angel, informs them that Jesus has been raised back to life, and he instructs the women to tell the disciples that they will see Jesus in Galilee (remember that Jesus died just outside of Jerusalem, in Judea). The women flee from the tomb in terror, and that's how the story ends (Mark 16:1–8).

Matthew's narrative is basically an expanded version of Mark's. There is now a guard at the tomb to make sure that nobody steals Jesus' body. When the women arrive, there's a great earthquake, and an angel unseals the tomb, which leaves the guards frozen in terror. The angel reveals that Jesus' body is gone and gives the women the same directive as in Mark. After leaving the tomb, the women encounter Jesus, who repeats the instruction to tell his disciples that they'll see him in Galilee. Meanwhile, the chief priests bribe the guards to say that the disciples stole Jesus' body. Later, in Galilee, the disciples meet Jesus on a mountain. They worship him there, but some have doubts (Matthew 28:1–20).

Luke's narrative starts on a similar note. A group of women, including Mary Magdalene, visit the tomb early Sunday morning with spices for Jesus' body. As in the other two accounts, they find the tomb unsealed and the body missing. Inside the tomb are two men, later identified as angels, who tell the women that Jesus has been raised back to life. However, the message of the angels is somewhat different here, and once the women leave the tomb, the narrative goes in an entirely different direction.

The women run off to tell the eleven disciples what they have seen, but the disciples don't believe them, so Peter runs to the tomb and confirms that it's empty. Then Jesus meets up with two other people while they're walking outside of Jerusalem. Although these people were followers of Jesus, they don't recognize him. Later, as they suddenly realize who he is, he vanishes from their sight. These two rejoin the eleven disciples in Jerusalem, who report that Jesus has now also appeared to Peter. While they are together, Jesus abruptly appears in their midst and proves that he's not a ghost by letting them touch his hands and feet, and by eating fish in their presence. He instructs them to wait in Jerusalem until God sends what he promised. Then they all go out to a nearby place called Bethany, where Jesus is taken up into heaven (Luke 24:1–53).

The narrative in John is also quite different from the others. Early on Sunday morning, Mary Magdalene goes to Jesus' tomb and finds it unsealed and empty. She runs to Peter and another disciple to inform them about the missing body. Peter and the other disciple run back to the tomb and confirm that it's empty. The disciples return to their homes (apparently without leaving Judea, even though they are from Galilee), while Mary stays behind at the tomb. First she sees two angels, and then she encounters Jesus, but she doesn't recognize him at first. When she finally realizes who he is, Jesus tells her to inform the disciples that he will be ascending to heaven. Later that evening, Jesus appears to the disciples behind locked doors, and he breathes on them to give them the Holy Spirit. Thomas is not present for the occasion and refuses to believe the other disciples when they tell him about it. A week later, Jesus appears to the whole group, and he encourages Thomas to feel his hands and side, where he still bears the marks of crucifixion. Thomas finally believes, and he acknowledges Jesus as his God (John 20:1–31).

The Gospel of John continues with a story about Jesus appearing to his disciples sometime later in Galilee. There's a miraculous catch of fish, after which the disciples eat breakfast with Jesus on shore. After breakfast, Jesus asks Peter if he loves him, and this leads into the exchange that we discussed much earlier in which Jesus is misunderstood as saying that the other disciple won't die until he returns (John 21:1–25).

Assessing the Sources

It seems impossible to harmonize the four resurrection narratives in any reasonable way. In Matthew's account, the disciples do not see Jesus until they return to Galilee, something which is also strongly implied by Mark. By contrast, all of Jesus' appearances in Luke's version of the story take place in or around Jerusalem, and Jesus specifically instructs the disciples not to leave the city. John is the only gospel where Jesus appears in both Jerusalem and Galilee.

It's important to appreciate that we can't just combine the narratives in order to resolve this discrepancy. Luke has altered his source material from Mark so that the women are no longer commanded to tell the disciples that they will see Jesus in Galilee. Instead, they are reminded of what Jesus said "while he was still in Galilee" (Luke 24:6). This is an intentional change on Luke's part. For reasons unknown, he has chosen to tell the story as if Jesus only appeared in the vicinity of Jerusalem.

The attempted harmonization also works against the inner logic of Matthew's account, where, once the disciples finally see Jesus in Galilee, some of them have doubts. Yet by this point, according to both Luke and John, they have already seen Jesus several times. Mashing the accounts together also completely destroys the logic of Jesus telling the women to let the disciples know that they will see him in Galilee, since he is apparently going to see them later that day in Jerusalem anyway.

Let's quickly mention a few more discrepancies:

- The first three gospels have the same sequence of events where the women visit the tomb, find it empty, have an angelic encounter, and leave. However, in John, Mary (who seems to be alone) does not see any angels until after she returns to the tomb a second time.

- In Luke, Peter does not examine the tomb for himself until after the women see the angels. But in John, Mary does not see the angels until after Peter checks the tomb.

- In John, Jesus gives the Holy Spirit to his disciples during his first appearance to them. However, the author of Luke does not have the disciples receiving the Holy Spirit until the day of Pentecost, after Jesus' ascension to heaven, which itself took place about forty days after his resurrection (Acts 2:1–13).

The discrepancies are important because they highlight areas where at least one of the accounts must be getting something wrong. This makes it clear that we cannot just take the resurrection narratives for granted, as if they were giving us a straightforward depiction of the events following Jesus' death (and given our earlier discussion of the gospels, this should come as no surprise).

Beyond this, there are other important reasons to approach the stories with caution. We know that at least some details in the narratives are plausibly understood as later Christian embellishments. For instance, in the accounts of Luke and John, Jesus goes out of his way to demonstrate that he is a physical being. This is often thought to reflect a later Christian emphasis on the fact that Jesus was a real human with a material body, against the teachings of those who said that Jesus only appeared to be human. (This is not to suggest that earlier Christians didn't believe in a physical resurrection, but only that, toward the end of the first century, the physical nature of Christ became a point of contention with certain other Christian groups.)

Still, even the embellishments provide us with some intriguing clues. For instance, Luke and John are clearly concerned to demonstrate that the empty tomb was verified by men. In the social world of the early Christians, to say that women were the first witnesses to the tomb was to invite scorn, since the testimony of women was widely thought to be less reliable than that of men. The fact that, in all four gospels, the empty tomb is discovered by a woman or group of women, and that, in two of them, women are the first ones to see Jesus alive, suggests that there may be an authentic historical core to the story. If Christian men in the first century were making the story up from scratch, one would expect it to look a bit different.

Equally important is Jesus' burial by Joseph of Arimathea. All four gospels agree that Joseph ensured Jesus' burial in a tomb. What makes this story surprising is that, according to Mark, he was "a respected member of the council," that is, the Judean council (Mark 15:43). This is the same council that handed Jesus over to Pilate to be killed.

Joseph's presence in the narrative is important. The early Christian movement clashed with the surrounding Jewish culture, and as time went on, hostility toward the Jewish people became more apparent in the Christian writings. It's one of the ugliest features of the New Testament. Matthew has "the people as a whole" begging Pilate to kill Jesus, shouting in unison, "His blood be on us and on our children" (Matthew 27:25). John often portrays people as being afraid of "the Jews" (John 7:13), and at one point Jesus tells his Jewish critics that their father is the Devil (John 8:44). So why would the early Christians make up a story about Jesus receiving an honorable burial from a member of the very council that condemned him for blasphemy?

This is not just a rhetorical question. There is good evidence that the authors of the gospels were uncomfortable with Joseph's role in the story. Matthew omits Mark's detail about Joseph being a member of the Judean council entirely, saying instead that he was a rich man "who also was himself a disciple of Jesus" (Matthew 27:57). Luke follows Mark in identifying Joseph as a member of the council, but calls him "a good and righteous man" who, "though a member of the council, had not agreed to their plan and action" (Luke 23:50–51). John takes the most deplorable approach, concurring with Matthew that Joseph was a disciple of Jesus, "though a secret one because of his fear of the Jews" (John 19:38). Mark himself may be saving face by claiming that Joseph was actually "waiting expectantly for the kingdom of God" (Mark 15:43).

All this discomfort with Joseph of Arimathea's involvement in Jesus' burial suggests that, had the authors of the gospels been able to remove him from the story, they would have. Jesus' burial by Joseph may have been familiar enough that sheer denial was impossible. This means that, if there were stories going around about Jesus' resurrection in the early days of the Christian movement, it may have been quite easy to locate his remains, had they still been present in their resting place. As far as we know, nobody ever took up this challenge.

Of course, this involves a certain amount of speculation, but when we combine the presence of Joseph of Arimathea with the earlier comments about the empty tomb being discovered by women, it results in an intriguing historical scenario. On the one hand, the stories of Jesus' resurrection are hopelessly irreconcilable and loaded with details that are hard to take seriously. On the other hand, it seems like there could be a tradition behind these stories that is firmly rooted in the memory of something that really happened.

The People Who Saw Jesus

By his own testimony, Paul was initially very hostile to the Christian community, to the point that he persecuted them and tried to destroy them (Galatians 1:13). After his experience of seeing Jesus, he became a Christian and suffered tremendously for his faith. In fact, he eventually died as a martyr, as did Peter and James.

The fact that the early Christians were persecuted for their faith is important to keep in mind, because it tells us that they were sincere in their convictions. Christians had little to gain from purposely spreading a lie. Even if Christianity later became the dominant religion of the empire, the early Christians did not yet have access to that kind of privilege. In light of these considerations, it is reasonable to think that Peter, Paul, and James were sincere in their conviction that they had seen Jesus alive.

When Paul names himself in the list of witnesses to Jesus' resurrection, he seems to regard his own experience of seeing Jesus as being unique in some way (see 1 Corinthians 15:8–9). However, he does not provide any details in his letters about what that experience entailed, beyond the claim that it was a direct revelation from God (Galatians 1:15–16). It is only later, in the book of Acts, that we find the story about Paul being blinded by a flash of light on the road to Damascus (Acts 9:1–19), but Paul never corroborates this narrative himself.

We know even less about the experiences of Peter, James, and the other disciples, since we don't have their direct testimony about it. It seems that the only hope we have for filling in the details of what these people actually saw is to rely on the conflicting reports of four writers from the late first century whose identities remain obscure. This poses obvious challenges.

Even if we try to focus exclusively on what the first three gospels seem to agree on, the results are quite meager: On the first day of the week, some women (including Mary Magdalene) went to Jesus' tomb, where they found his body missing. At the tomb they encountered one or two angels, and some time later, the disciples saw Jesus. The end. With Paul's list of witnesses, we can at least corroborate that Jesus was seen by Peter and the other disciples, and that he was seen sometimes by individuals, and other times by groups. The appearances seem to have been intermittent, but anything else we might say about them would be speculative. It would be nice if we could say more, but because of the discrepancies (to say nothing of the questionable credibility of the sources), it is difficult to put much confidence in any specific details.

The Empty Tomb

Apologists frequently claim that the disciples would never have come to believe in Jesus' resurrection on the basis of the appearances alone, but only if they had also personally known Jesus' tomb to be empty. In this way, the mere fact that the disciples came to believe that Jesus had been raised indicates that they really must have known that his tomb was vacant. This, in turn, is used to support the claim that God really did raise Jesus back to life.[2]

Now, maybe Jesus' tomb really was found empty, but Paul seems to have converted to Christianity entirely on the basis of what he took to be a personal encounter with Jesus. Paul is famously silent on the subject of Jesus' tomb. The fact that he doesn't mention it may indicate that it wasn't all that important to him. If Paul's faith in Jesus' resurrection didn't require him to believe that Jesus' tomb had been found empty, then we have no grounds for assuming that such a thing would have been essential for the faith of any other first-century Christians.

Remember, there is a difference between believing that Jesus' body was raised back to life and believing that witnesses saw an empty tomb with their own eyes. I think it's clear from Paul's letters that he believed that Jesus' physical body had been raised and transformed, and thus I am quite sure that Paul believed that, after Jesus' resurrection, his tomb was no longer occupied. But this doesn't mean that Paul knew of any stories about the tomb being discovered empty. We just don't know if Paul proclaimed the discovery of the empty tomb, since he never mentions it. And my point is that, in spite of what so many Christian apologists have argued, it's not even remotely obvious that the discovery of an empty tomb would have been necessary for convincing any of Jesus' disciples that he had been raised back to life.

Some scholars who prefer a more liberal form of Christianity see the empty tomb as irrelevant to the resurrection. For them, resurrection is not something that concerns Jesus' physical body at all. Instead, they see it as a metaphor which means both that "Jesus lives" and that "Jesus is

Lord."[3] This approach is heavily based on a confused reading of Paul's discussion of the resurrection body in 1 Corinthians 15, but we do not need to sort through the details of that difficult passage in order to see why this metaphorical approach does not work.

First, it's not clear what it means to say that Jesus is the risen Lord if his body rotted away and if the man we call Jesus of Nazareth remained dead. In spite of claims to the contrary, this really is just a denial of resurrection, not an affirmation of it. One may see in Jesus an ideal picture of a godly life, or one may have a vaguely defined spiritual experience centered around Jesus, but this has no connection to the ancient Jewish concept of resurrection, which involved empty graves and the restoration of bodily life.

Second, scholars who interpret Jesus' resurrection and ascension as metaphors undermine their own position by also affirming that the early Christians believed in a literal second coming.[4] Paul certainly expected Jesus to return from heaven in a literal sense. It makes no sense to suppose that the early Christians believed in a metaphorical resurrection and a literal second coming, since the literal, physical return from heaven of a man who died seems to require some kind of literal, physical resurrection. Thus, when the early Christians said that God raised Jesus back to life, they must have meant it quite literally.

This seems like a good place to voice my own concerns about the empty tomb. On the one hand, I think that the burial by Joseph of Arimathea and the discovery of the tomb by women both lend great plausibility to the claim that Jesus' body really was missing. On the other hand, I have some nagging doubts.

Part of it concerns the strange way that Mark ends his gospel. He explicitly says that the women were frightened and didn't tell anybody what they had seen (Mark 16:8). For the life of me, I cannot understand why Mark would end his gospel this way if he meant to suggest that the women did, in fact, end up telling people what they had seen. Now, by itself this would just be an odd historical curiosity. But given the fact that earlier Christian sources do not talk about an empty tomb being discovered, one wonders if Mark is trying to make a point here. Is he saying that nobody talked about the empty tomb until now because the women who discovered it didn't tell anyone? Is there an implied acknowledgement that Christians didn't start telling the story of the empty tomb until decades after Jesus' death? And is Mark being misogynistic by blaming it on the women? I don't think the evidence requires us to think this way, but that doesn't mean the scenario is implausible.

Arguments that the women's silence was obviously short-lived ("It *had* to be a temporary silence; otherwise Mark couldn't be telling the story about it!") seem not to take the question seriously at all.[5] Nor does it help to appeal to other cases in Mark where Jesus commands people not to say anything, but then they do it anyway (Mark 1:43–45). The obvious difference here is that the women were not commanded to be silent, and they are not, after all, depicted as saying anything to anybody. It is notable in this context that Matthew, in order to make his own version of the story work (since he has the women running to tell the disciples what happened), has to omit the comment that the women said nothing to anyone (see Matthew 28:8). A narrative where the women say nothing to anyone but then say something to someone is quite obviously incoherent. So Mark's ending remains a real puzzle for honest inquirers.

Furthermore, even though the discovery of the empty tomb by women is obviously very significant, I wonder if its significance has been overstated. It is often said that the women were already omitted from the story by the time of Paul's oral tradition because of male chauvinism. However, the early Christian communities are known to have been surprisingly egalitarian, since women were allowed to publicly pray and prophesy in the assembly (1 Corinthians 11:5), and Paul recognizes women as apostles and deacons (Romans 16:1, 7). This was not by any means a matter of indifference for Paul, since he explicitly declares that, in Christ, "there is no longer male and female" (Galatians 3:28).

It is true, of course, that Paul's letters contain some of the most infamous misogynistic passages found in the entire Bible. But most of these passages appear in letters (Ephesians, Colossians, 1 Timothy) that were probably not actually written by Paul; they are most likely pseudonymous.[6] The only relevant passage which appears in an authentic letter (1 Corinthians 14:34–35) is often thought to be a later addition from someone other than Paul, based partially on the fact that different manuscripts have the words appearing in different places.

My point is not to deny the possibility of misogyny in early Christianity, but to observe that the evidence is not as clear-cut as it is often made out to be. I am just not fully convinced that the women would *necessarily* have been screened out of the earliest Christian oral traditions on chauvinistic grounds. Perhaps their absence from these traditions stems from the fact that the empty tomb story hadn't been invented yet.

There are other related issues that we could explore here, but I don't want to belabor the point, especially since the discovery of the empty tomb remains plausible and I am sincerely open-minded about it. I neither affirm it nor deny it, but simply remain an agnostic.

Explaining the Relevant Facts

In light of our discussion so far, we can generate a small list of facts which are relevant to the topic of Jesus' resurrection. First, after his death, Jesus was buried in a sealed tomb.[7] Second, the disciples and Paul had experiences in which they saw (or at least, they believed that they saw) Jesus alive after his death. Third, Paul was a former enemy of the Christian movement whose experience transformed him so profoundly that he became a believer and ended up dying for his faith. Fourth, the appearances of Jesus were intermittent. Fifth, the early Christians explained all of this in terms of Jesus' resurrection. In other words, it was not a legend that took decades to materialize. Sixth, Jesus is no longer present in the world as he was before he died (this may seem almost too obvious to mention, but its importance will become evident later on). Finally, we may add a potential seventh fact: sometime after his burial, Jesus' body disappeared from its resting place.

But now we want to consider the question of what actually happened. In other words, we are looking for the best way to explain the relevant historical facts. So what is it, exactly, that makes for a "best" explanation? There are a number of factors, and I will mention four that are especially important for our purposes. First, the explanation must have *greater explanatory scope* than other theories, meaning that it accounts for a wider variety of known facts. Second, it must have *greater explanatory power* than other theories, meaning that it does a better job of making the known facts more probable than they would have been otherwise. Third, it must be *more plausible* than other theories, meaning that it is implied by a greater number of accepted truths. Fourth, it must be *less ad hoc* than rival theories, meaning that it asks us to make fewer new assumptions that are not required by the data.[8]

Many Christian scholars are convinced that the best way to account for the data of Jesus' postmortem appearances and his empty tomb is by positing that he really did rise from the dead. Certainly, an empty tomb and a series of postmortem appearances seem far more probable on the supposition that God raised Jesus from the dead than on the assumption that Jesus stayed dead. But what about alternative theories? The reader may be surprised to learn that, among those scholars who deny the resurrection, there is no consensus about what caused the emergence of Christian faith.

It's easy to miss the significance of this point. Sometimes people seem to think that *any* theory could get the job done. For example, one might suppose that Jesus survived his crucifixion, and that his followers somehow mistook this for a resurrection. However, off-the-cuff speculation like this often reflects a failure to take the historical question seriously enough. After all, it's highly unlikely that Jesus survived his execution, since Roman soldiers certainly knew how to kill a man, and crucifixion was not the sort of thing that a person could just walk away from. Furthermore, how could a savagely beaten crucifixion victim convince his followers that he had conquered death? And why is there no record of Jesus continuing to live out the rest of his days after his crucifixion? Where did he go? Did he retire and move to Florida?

Don't get me wrong. It's easy enough to come up with a theory to explain any particular event. For instance, it seems perfectly possible that religious fervor and the power of suggestion could have played a role in causing some people to think they had seen Jesus. But getting a theory that accounts for all the data at once is more challenging. Would religious fervor and the power of suggestion account for Paul's experience? By his own testimony, Paul was an enemy to the early Christian movement. How suggestible would he really have been? If anything, he probably had a strong bias *against* believing in Jesus.

Maybe we can explain Paul by supposing that he felt guilty about persecuting Christians. Perhaps he had a positive or redemptive experience with a Christian whose life he tried to destroy, and maybe this caused him to have a change of heart. It could be that, in light of this experience, he became more suggestible and thus more prone to seeing Jesus.

But what about the empty tomb (assuming that the tomb really was empty)? Religious fervor, the power of suggestion, and deep feelings of guilt aren't enough to make a body disappear. Well, okay then. Perhaps Jesus' body was stolen by grave robbers. Grave robbery was a real problem in those days, and the body of a miracle worker would have had great appeal to certain thieves. However, once we appeal to grave robbery, we no longer have any way to explain the appearances of Jesus.

Of course, we could always combine several theories together. Maybe the origin of Christian faith stems from a combination of religious fervor, suggestibility, guilt, and grave robbers. This meets the requirement of explanatory scope. Notice, though, that each component of this theory is already highly speculative. We have gone far beyond the evidence. When we start piling one speculative theory on top of another, the resulting combination becomes far less probable, and far more ad hoc. It *could* be what happened, but it could just as easily have been some other unlikely combination of events, a point which is not lost on Christian apologists.[9] The current evidence does not compel us to embrace any particular historical reconstruction—and that is just the problem.

The Resurrection Hypothesis

Christian apologists often make triumphant claims about the success of the historical argument for Jesus' resurrection. After all, why resort to speculation about religious fervor and grave robbery when there's an elegantly simple theory at hand that can explain all of the data easily, in one fell swoop? Wouldn't it be much simpler to believe in Jesus' resurrection and call it a day? I used to think so, but then I realized that the resurrection hypothesis faces its own major problems. I can think of at least five.

Problem #1: The Concept of Resurrection

The appeal to Jesus' resurrection cannot even get off the ground unless we understand what *resurrection* is supposed to mean, but when we stop to consider this question, we discover a fair amount of confusion. If we simply mean that Jesus came back to life, then his resurrection explains almost nothing. It does not explain why his appearances to the disciples and Paul were intermittent, or why they eventually stopped. It does not even explain how he got out of his sealed tomb.

Before diving into the real heart of this issue, let's make sure we have a firm grasp on what the discussion is about. Suppose that a Christian says, "Obviously, Jesus was able to leave his tomb because the angel rolled the stone away." Why doesn't this objection work? The reason is that it misunderstands both the historical problem and the nature of the resurrection hypothesis itself.

The historical problem is that we have a set of relevant facts that call out for an explanation. We have already seen why the gospel narratives cannot be taken for granted—this is precisely why the historical problem exists. If we could just take the angel's presence at the tomb for granted, then there would be no historical problem to speak of.

As a result, we don't actually know if there really were angels at Jesus' tomb or not. So we cannot just solve the historical problem by assuming that an angel moved the stone. If we want to, we can work the angel into our hypothesis and see how it holds up.

However, the angel is not part of the resurrection hypothesis. Why not? Because the purpose of the resurrection hypothesis is to provide a reasonable, principled evaluation of the evidence, and only after this hypothesis is accepted can we build a theological framework on top of it. If we start invoking angels in order to supplement the resurrection hypothesis, then we are making additional theological assumptions that are not necessarily required by the data.

In fact, only one source (Matthew) claims that it was an angel who moved the stone, and one could easily see this as an embellishment of the earlier source material. As a result, the resurrection-plus-angel theory suffers from being too ad hoc. It presupposes too much of what the argument for the resurrection is meant to prove in the first place. (Incidentally, I am not aware of any apologist who appeals to angels in arguing for the resurrection.)

Now we can return to the point I raised. If Jesus simply came back to life, then we are left without any explanation of how he got out of his tomb or how he was able to appear to people in an intermittent fashion. What Christian apologists typically say, then, is that Jesus came back to life in some kind of transformed, glorified state. This would allegedly explain why Jesus was able to appear and disappear at will, and why he could sometimes be seen by those who knew him without being recognized. Apologists often present this idea as if it were just part of what it means to say that Jesus was raised from the dead.

However, the source material does not seem to justify this claim. There are stories in the gospels where Jesus brings other dead people back to life, including one in which the restored person, a man named Lazarus, is described as having been "raised from the dead" (John 12:9). Yet these other resurrected folks do not seem to have enjoyed the same powers that Jesus did after he came back to life. They could not (as far as we are told) appear and disappear at will or suddenly materialize behind locked doors. The Lazarus story is a particularly interesting case because, in spite of being raised from the dead, he still needs assistance with having his tomb unsealed and getting out of his burial clothes (John 11:39, 44). Now, perhaps Christian apologists do not accept these other stories as bona fide cases of resurrection. Sometimes Christian writers use the word *resuscitation* to refer to bringing a dead person back to life, in order to draw a contrast between that and resurrection. In any case, apologists are offering Jesus' resurrection as a unique event that necessarily entails that his body was transformed.

Unfortunately, this does not help the hypothesis very much, because the notion of *transformation*, in this context, is considerably vague. Transformed into what? Apologists frequently appeal to Paul's letters, since he claims that, after the resurrection, Jesus' body was glorified and no longer subject to decay or corruption (see 1 Corinthians 15:35–55). But glorification is an ambiguous concept as well, and Paul does not give any indication that this gives a person the ability to dematerialize and rematerialize at will.

To say that people whose bodies are transformed and glorified can do the types of things that Jesus did after his resurrection is a mere assertion, but what is it grounded in? If the answer is to say that people who are glorified can do these things because Jesus did them and he was glorified, then we are reasoning in a circle. It seems that we are cooking up a special definition of *glorification* for this one specific occasion.

This makes the resurrection hypothesis quite a bit more ad hoc than its proponents care to admit. To be sure, the early Christians appealed to different theological concepts in order to make sense of what they believed had happened to Jesus. But these concepts do not provide any explanation for why Jesus could just disappear and reappear in different locations. So to claim that the data can be explained by the hypothesis of resurrection is simply incorrect, unless we have some prior independent grounds for saying that resurrection is consistent with the ability to instantaneously vanish and transport oneself from place to place. However, I am not aware of any such grounds.

As a last-ditch effort, the apologist could say that Jesus' new abilities were simply due to the power of God, and thus they are irrelevant to the resurrection itself. After all, the book of Acts claims that, at one point, the Holy Spirit instantly "snatched" the apostle Philip and dropped him off over twenty miles away (see Acts 8:39–40). This event surely had nothing to do with Philip being resurrected or glorified. Not only that, but Jesus, by the power of the Holy Spirit or by his own divine nature, could already do a number of spectacular things even before his death, such as walking on water. So what's the problem with saying that Jesus did some peculiar things after his resurrection?

The problem is that the resurrection hypothesis is supposed to be an evidential argument which, on its own terms, explains the historical data in a satisfying way, giving us a reason to accept the Christian view of Jesus. But now it seems that, in order for the hypothesis to get off the ground, one already has to accept quite a number of Christian beliefs about Jesus to begin with, including his spectacular miracles and divine power, and perhaps the reliability of the gospels and the book of Acts. If we don't begin with these beliefs, we are left with the bare concept of *resurrection* which, by itself, cannot explain (unless it is reworked in an ad hoc fashion) how Jesus got out of his tomb and popped up randomly in different places.

The apologist who wants to make an evidential case for the resurrection of Jesus cannot simply appeal to questionable theological data from the New Testament in order to rehabilitate their hypothesis. Since nobody accepts the New Testament as a reliable theological resource who isn't already a Christian believer, the integrity of this data is part of what is being debated when we ask if Jesus' resurrection really took place. In short, the resurrection hypothesis suffers from being too ad hoc.

Problem #2: The Appearances

The second problem with the resurrection hypothesis is that its explanatory power is questionable when it comes to the appearances of Jesus. Remember, it needs to do a better job of making the appearances of Jesus more probable than any other theory would. And at first glance, this seems like a no-brainer: "Of course it's more probable that the disciples and Paul would see Jesus, given his resurrection, than if he had not been raised!" But ask yourself, what does it *mean* that the disciples and Paul saw Jesus?

We have already seen why we can't just take the gospel narratives for granted. While conflicting sources can obviously yield historical truth, the problem here is that the narratives diverge in such fundamental ways that it is not clear which details related to the appearances we would be justified in accepting.

As we saw earlier, Matthew and Mark strongly imply that Jesus was not seen by his disciples until they were back in Galilee, without narrating or suggesting any other appearances to them. Luke only talks about Jerusalem-based appearances, and he does so in a way that seems to rule out the Galilee appearances. John says that the disciples saw Jesus first in Jerusalem and then later in Galilee. In light of these differences, Christian apologists are surely claiming far more than is warranted when they infer that Jesus was seen first in Jerusalem, then in Galilee, and again (later) in Jerusalem.[10] One cannot determine which appearances took place, and where, unless one already makes an arbitrary decision to accept certain parts of the narratives as reliable while ignoring their other details. To claim that these aren't real discrepancies is to give up on taking this topic seriously.

As a result, there are lots of important questions about the appearances of Jesus that we can't answer, such as: *Were they fleeting glimpses or prolonged sightings? Did the disciples really interact with Jesus in these experiences? Who claimed to have seen him first, and how did others react to this? Did everyone see the same thing? Were some of the appearances drastically different from the others? Did the witnesses disagree on any important points? Did any of the witnesses need to be coerced into agreeing with others about what had happened? Did any of the disciples remain skeptical?*

One problem with our limited data, then, is that we just don't know exactly what kind of phenomenon we're trying to explain. It is pointless to assert that the appearances of Jesus were "physical" and "bodily" on the grounds of what Paul says in his discussion of the resurrection body in 1 Corinthians 15, since this is part of Paul's interpretation of the resurrection of Jesus, but not a description of what he saw.[11] He obviously believed that Jesus possessed a real immortal body, but so what? This does not provide any insight as to what the experience of seeing Jesus entailed. Again, if we just arbitrarily assume that it must have been something like what we find in the gospel narratives, then we are not really taking the historical question seriously enough.

At this point, the question of what could *possibly* have caused the disciples to see (or think they saw) Jesus must be considered. Normally, apologists approach this in a somewhat simplistic fashion by limiting our options to hallucinations, visions, or sightings of an objective, mind-independent reality. They argue that if we can rule out hallucinations and visions, then the disciples must have seen a mind-independent reality, and this can only be explained by appealing to Jesus' resurrection.

For this reason, Christian apologists often make much of the fact that Paul cites an appearance to more than five hundred people at once in his list of witnesses. This detail, in an early tradition, is sometimes viewed as ironclad proof that the appearances of Jesus were not hallucinations or visions, since these are subjective experiences that cannot be shared between individuals. Since five hundred people couldn't all have had the same hallucination, it *must* be the case that they all really saw Jesus.[12]

But who are these five hundred mystery guests? We don't even know their names. Even worse, in this case we don't have any gospel narratives to help us out. What exactly did this mass sighting of Jesus entail? Was he close to them, or did they see him standing far away? Did he say anything? Or was it a brief flash?

I'm reminded of the strange, physically impossible behavior of the sun witnessed by thousands of people in Fatima, Portugal on October 13, 1917, apparently in fulfillment of a prediction that allegedly came from the Virgin Mary herself.[13] A Catholic miracle witnessed by tens of thousands of people seems significant. If you're like me, you'll think, "That sounds interesting, but how could I possibly know what really happened? I wasn't there."

It would be hard, of course, to dismiss the event as a mere hallucination or vision, since it was a group occurrence—and what a large group! But I doubt that many Protestant apologists will feel a burden to convert to Catholicism on the grounds that it must have been something real. Nor would I blame them, except in regard to their lack of consistency. Thus, the testimony of five hundred unnamed individuals who witnessed a sighting of Jesus that we know nothing else about turns out to be quite useless in terms of evidence.

Additionally, there are certain striking parallels between the reports of Jesus' appearances and the multitude of reports concerning apparitions of recently deceased people. This doesn't mean that we have to believe in ghosts (that is certainly not the point I am making), but these stories are reported across a wide variety of cultures and all throughout history, including in modern contexts where beliefs about the supernatural are often discouraged, and some of the cases are very well documented.

In many cases, these apparitions are not just seen but also heard. They are seen at different times by different people, and sometimes by multiple people at once. They often speak briefly, not usually more than a couple sentences, and provide guidance or make requests. To those who experience them, the apparitions can seem not just real but solid, and they appear and disappear in abrupt, unusual ways. Reports of apparitions of a recently deceased person also tend to decrease as time goes on.[14]

Interestingly, my mother had an experience like this when she was a young girl. Sometime around Easter of 1963, she awoke one night to see her grandfather sitting in her bedroom. It seemed real enough to her that she did not feel alarmed at all, and she went back to sleep. The next morning she shared this with her mother, assuming that her grandfather was visiting. Her mother informed her that her grandfather had not come to visit, and that he had passed away the night before. My mother has never been particularly superstitious when it comes to ghost stories, and the few times I've ever heard her talk about this experience, she has not offered any theories about what it all means. It's just an odd thing that happened once.

The skeptic of the resurrection is certainly not burdened with figuring out exactly how or why these events happen; rather, it's enough to acknowledge that apparitions of the deceased are a widely reported phenomenon, whereas resurrections are not. This raises the possibility that those who saw Jesus after his death were having a similar kind of experience, which they misinterpreted as evidence that Jesus had been raised back to life. So for the resurrection hypothesis to have better explanatory power than all other theories, we would need to differentiate between what the disciples experienced and what other people typically experience when they see or hear apparitions of recently deceased persons. But this is precisely where our data fails us. It's not just because we have no way to know what the disciples' experiences entailed, but also because the general phenomenon of apparitions of the deceased is a significant, perplexing mystery in its own right.

Apologists frequently object that ghost stories have been around for a long time, and that, if the sightings of Jesus were just "conventional" apparitions, the disciples would have taken it as evidence that he was dead, not that he was alive.[15] In other words, those who experience apparitions of the deceased typically do not conclude that the person they saw was raised from the dead, providing a crucial disanalogy between the appearances of Jesus and other apparitions.[16] However, this objection fails for two reasons.

First, it is undercut by the belief of most Christian apologists that Jesus predicted his death and resurrection several times before he died. If the predictions are authentic (and personally I have no strong opinion one way or the other), then the disciples had every reason to anticipate the fulfillment of his words. In that case, it would create theological space for them to interpret apparitions (or even subjective visions) of Jesus as proof that a resurrection had occurred, something which does not exist in other cases where people see a recently deceased person.

Second, even if we disregard the predictions as later Christian inventions, the objection still ignores the impact that Jesus must have had on the disciples' thinking before he died. Not only did they associate

Jesus' ministry with the expectation that the end was near, but they also believed that he was the Messiah, which (like resurrection) was an "end times" concept. It's true that they probably knew of stories about apparitions of the dead, but this doesn't mean that they were personally acquainted with what these experiences look or feel like. So it seems perfectly plausible that the experience of seeing Jesus after his death, in what appeared to be a healthy and powerful form (whatever that experience actually entailed), would encourage them to think in terms of resurrection, given the way that Jesus taught them to view the world.

For these reasons, I don't think we are in a position to say that the resurrection of Jesus has superior (or even adequate) explanatory power without knowing more about the details of what the disciples and Paul actually experienced. And we can't put much stock in the narratives in the gospels because of their disagreements and embellishments. So I am just as unmoved when hearing about the appearances of Jesus as I am when I hear about the events that supposedly occurred at Fatima. We need more to go on than just a few bare facts, intriguing as they may be.

Problem #3: An Incomplete Theory

Contrary to what Christian apologists claim, the resurrection fails to account for all of the relevant data, and thus it lacks adequate explanatory scope. There is one glaring detail that the resurrection, by itself, does not explain: the absence of Jesus. Why isn't Jesus still around?

On the traditional Christian view, he only stuck around for a limited period of time, and then he ascended to heaven in full view of his disciples. In spite of what apologists may think about combination theories, their own theory is quite extravagant in this regard. Their historical hypothesis is not just resurrection, but resurrection plus glorification plus ascension.

Problem #4: The Implausibility of the Ascension

The ascension seriously undermines whatever credibility the resurrection hypothesis had to begin with. For one thing, the doctrine of the ascension seems to reflect a pre-scientific view of the world, since we're meant to believe that Jesus literally ascended upward to heaven. Not only that, but believing that the disciples actually witnessed the ascension depends entirely on accepting the sole testimony of Luke, an anonymous, late first-century writer who never even claimed to have met Jesus.

I suppose we could deny that Jesus' ascension is meant to be taken literally, as some apologists have done,[17] but then we have to throw out the testimony of Luke, who explicitly states that the disciples were left looking up into the sky after Jesus lifted off the ground and disappeared behind a cloud (Acts 1:9–10). In that case, there's no reason to think that anyone witnessed Jesus' ascension in the first place.

The result is that the resurrection hypothesis becomes more ad hoc, since it's only tacking on the ascension hypothesis for the sake of theological convenience, and not because the evidence demands it. But without the ascension, Christians are left with no way to explain why the risen Jesus went missing two thousand years ago.

Problem #5: The Theological Context

Christian apologists insist that we interpret a miracle like the resurrection in light of the context of Jesus' ministry, but it is precisely this context which makes his resurrection seem so profoundly unlikely. If we take Jesus' false proclamation about the imminent final judgment seriously (and why on earth shouldn't we?), then it becomes very difficult to think that God raised him back to life after he died. Why would God resurrect a man who is, by his own standards, a false prophet?

Of course, if God exists, God can do whatever God wants. But if we're trying to form the best explanation of the evidence, then resurrection seems like the wrong way to go. After all, in a Christian framework, the resurrection is supposed to be the ultimate vindication of Jesus. Yet if Jesus' message was heavily based on a false proclamation about God, then what exactly does the resurrection vindicate? How can it give us a solid basis for faith? What are we supposed to think about the risen Jesus if we know that his teachings lack credibility?

The Resurrection Hypothesis: A Final Assessment

At this point, a Christian apologist could possibly concede everything I've said. They could admit that their resurrection hypothesis is really a combination of resurrection plus glorification plus ascension, and perhaps admit that, as of yet, they don't know what to make of Jesus' false predictions. But even in spite of all of this, they might continue to say that their resurrection hypothesis is still the best explanation of the data available, since no other hypothesis appears to get the job done.

I have two responses to this. First, if the resurrection theory is an ad hoc combination theory which relies on heavy speculation (since we have to simply assume, without evidence, that there *must* be a way to resolve the false predictions, in addition to all the other strange theological assumptions this theory requires), then it seems no better to me than speculating about a combination of non-miraculous causes. If anything, it seems worse, since there's no good way to make sense of why God would raise Jesus back to life, only to take him away for thousands of years, particularly since this long, unexplained absence only undermines Jesus' credibility as a prophet.

Second, it seems to me that in order for any hypothesis to qualify as the "best" historical explanation (meaning that we are justified in accepting it as the truth), it has to be a good explanation. That is to say, we don't typically settle for poor explanations just because there's no other explanation available.

Here is an example from my own life: Once, when I was home alone, I saw a pile of laundry seemingly push itself out into the hallway from the room I used as a home office. I had no pets at the time, all the doors were locked, I was fully awake and alert, and it happened right before my eyes. In fact, the incident took place while I was talking to a friend on the phone, and I commented on what was happening as it happened.

My first, most natural thought was: "Oh, I had the laundry in a pile on the computer chair, it must have fallen off." Then I remembered that the chair was across the room from the door, which I promptly confirmed. It was too far away for the laundry to have made the trip to the hallway just by falling. Could it have somehow been blown across the room? It did not seem likely. The fans were all off and the windows were all closed, and I had never felt a draft in that room before, nor could I detect one at the moment. So that couldn't be it.

My next thought was more troubling. I have an intense (admittedly irrational) fear of rats, so I immediately panicked at the thought that a rat had somehow gotten into my house and was pushing the laundry around. But then I grabbed a broom and soon confirmed that the laundry pile was empty, and there was no rat (or any other living creature for that matter) to move it around. Another dead end.

Some of my friends drew a more obvious (if not superstitious) conclusion: My house must be haunted, and it was a ghost that moved the laundry. Honestly, after exhausting all other possibilities, I wondered if this could really be the case. But even apart from my general skepticism about ghosts, this explanation never really made sense to me either. For one thing, I never experienced any other spooky activity in that house before or after the laundry incident. And in spite of how creepy the unfinished basement looked, I can honestly say that I never once felt creeped out by being alone in that house (not even during the laundry incident). Additionally, even if I wanted to believe in ghosts, I can't make any sense of why a ghost would bother to move a small pile of laundry in my house on a single occasion and then call it a day. Not a very effective poltergeist, if you ask me.

In short, the laundry incident remains an unsolved mystery. And in fact, there are a great number of unsolved mysteries on the books (there even used to be a whole TV show dedicated to them). In cases like these, we do not just arbitrarily pick whatever explanation we can, as long as it seems better to us than its rivals. Instead, we simply say that we haven't got a good explanation yet, and so the question of what really happened remains open. We might have different theories—I still think that my laundry must have fallen out of the chair and tumbled in an extremely improbable way, and some of my friends still think it was a ghost—but we are not justified in presenting any of them as "what probably happened," because we simply have no way to know.

At this point, I can imagine one final objection from the Christian apologist. They might point out that, whenever detectives face an un-solved mystery, they don't just give up and go home. Rather, if they're doing their jobs correctly, they follow every lead and test every plausible theory they can think of. So in the case of the resurrection of Jesus, it would be methodologically unsound to abandon the theory just because of a few loose ends.

In response to this, I want to make it clear that I am not encouraging anyone to just ignore the resurrection hypothesis. That certainly isn't what I've been doing in this book. I think it's a fascinating topic that merits our attention. But if we want to take the hypothesis seriously as a potential explanation for the relevant historical data, then we can't just put the theory up on the board and declare victory. We've got to test it rigorously to see if it fits with the evidence. And the problem is that the theory that God raised Jesus back to life simply breaks down in light of this testing process. Thus, when it comes to Jesus' resurrection, I remain skeptical on both historical and theological grounds. As for what really happened, we can only speculate.

It's disappointing, of course, to be denied a satisfying explanation of what really happened after Jesus died. Sir Arthur Conan Doyle added some realism to his stories about the great detective Sherlock Holmes by writing that some cases "baffled his analytical skill, and would be, as narratives, beginnings without an ending."[18] Unfortunately, when it comes to solving the mystery of Jesus' postmortem appearances, we find ourselves facing a similar prospect. The evidence is tantalizing, but we seem to be left, inescapably, without an ending.

Endnotes

Preface

1. Lee Strobel, *The Case for Christ: A Journalist's Personal Investigation of the Evidence for Jesus* (Grand Rapids, MI: Zondervan, 1998).

The Son of God

1. Compare to 1 Samuel 21:1–6.

False Prophecies

1. Romans, 1 Corinthians, 2 Corinthians, Galatians, Philippians, 1 Thessalonians, Philemon.

2. Norman L. Geisler and Thomas Howe, *The Big Book of Bible Difficulties: Clear and Concise Answers from Genesis to Revelation* (Grand Rapids, MI: Baker Books, 2008), 358–59.

3. Ibid., 359.

4. Robert H. Stein, *Jesus, the Temple, and the Coming of the Son of Man: A Commentary on Mark 13* (Downers Grove, IL: IVP Academic, 2014), 125–27.

5. Kenneth L. Barker et al, eds., *Zondervan NIV Study Bible*, rev. ed. (Grand Rapids: Zondervan, 2002), 1496n16:28.

6. N. T. Wright, *Jesus and the Victory of God* (Minneapolis, MN: Fortress Press, 1996), 320–68.

7. William Lane Craig, "Was Jesus a Failed Eschatological Prophet?" *Reasonable Faith*, November 25, 2013, https://www.reasonablefaith.org/writings/question-answer/was-jesus-a-failed-eschatological-prophet.

8. Ibid.

9. Christopher M. Hays, et al., *When the Son of Man Didn't Come: A Constructive Proposal on the Delay of the Parousia* (Minneapolis, MN: Fortress Press, 2016).

The Gospels

1. *Against Heresies* III.I.1.

2. Papias is quoted in Eusebius, *Church History* III.39.1–7, 15–16.

3. Michael W. Holmes, *The Apostolic Fathers in English*, 3rd ed. (Grand Rapids, MI: Baker Academic, 2006), 316.

4. For example, see 1 Clement 13:1.

5. *Dialogue with Trypho* 106.

6. Craig A. Evans, *Jesus and the Manuscripts: What We Can Learn from the Oldest Texts* (Peabody, MA: Hendrickson Academic, 2020), 33–51.

7. For a good discussion, see Adela Yarbro Collins, *Mark: A Commentary*, ed. Harold W. Attridge (Minneapolis, MN: Fortress Press, 2007), 2–6.

8. See Bart D. Ehrman, *Forgery and Counterforgery: The Use of Literary Deceit in Early Christian Polemics* (Oxford: Oxford University Press, 2013), 265–76.

9. Michael R. Licona, *Why Are There Differences in the Gospels? What We Can Learn from Ancient Biography* (New York: Oxford University Press, 2017), 130.

10. Lee Strobel, *The Case for the Real Jesus: A Journalist Investigates Current Attacks on the Identity of Christ* (Grand Rapids, MI: Zondervan, 2007), 59.

11. Elizabeth Williamson, *Sandy Hook: An American Tragedy and the Battle for Truth* (n.p.: Dutton, 2022).

12. Dale C. Allison, Jr., *The Resurrection of Jesus: Apologetics, Polemics, History* (New York: Bloomsbury, 2021), 181–82.

13. Lee Strobel, *The Case for Christ: A Journalist's Personal Investigation of the Evidence for Jesus* (Grand Rapids, MI: Zondervan, 1998), 45.

14. Ibid., 27–28.

15. The manuscripts for 1:41 differ on whether Jesus was moved with anger or compassion.

16. William Lane Craig, *Reasonable Faith: Christian Truth and Apologetics*, 3rd ed. (Wheaton, IL: Crossway, 2008), 312.

17. Licona, *Why Are There Differences in the Gospels*, 165–66.

18. Collins, *Mark*, 353.

19. E. P. Sanders, *The Historical Figure of Jesus* (London: Penguin Books, 1995), 219–20.

What Jesus Believed

1. *Antiquities of the Jews* XX.9.1.

2. Dale C. Allison Jr., *Constructing Jesus: Memory, Imagination, and History* (Grand Rapids, MI: Baker Academic, 2010), 33n10.

3. Compare to 2 Kings 1:8.

4. John Dominic Crossan, *The Historical Jesus: The Life of a Mediterranean Jewish Peasant* (New York: HarperOne, 1991), 237–8.

5. Allison, *Constructing Jesus*, 85–6.

Liars and Lunatics

1. C. S. Lewis, *Mere Christianity*, in *The C. S. Lewis Signature Classics* (New York: HarperOne, 2017), 50–52.

2. Ibid., 50.

3. Compare to Psalm 107:23–29.

4. William Lane Craig, *Reasonable Faith: Christian Truth and Apologetics*, 3rd ed. (Wheaton, IL: Crossway, 2008), 315–19.

5. Bart D. Ehrman, *Did Jesus Exist? The Historical Argument for Jesus of Nazareth* (New York: HarperOne, 2012), 305–07.

6. 1QS 9:3–11.

7. Josephus, *Antiquities of the Jews* 20.8.6.

Miracles

1. David Hume, *An Enquiry Concerning Human Understanding*, Kindle e-book (Digireads.com, 2011), 107.

2. Bart D. Ehrman, *Jesus, Interrupted: Revealing the Hidden Contradictions in the Bible (and Why We Don't Know About Them)* (New York: HarperOne, 2009), 176.

3. Ibid., 177.

4. C. Thomas Anderson, *Becoming a Millionaire God's Way: Getting money to you, not from you* (Phoenix, AZ: Winword Publishing, 2004), 3.

5. Elizabeth F. Loftus, *Eyewitness Testimony* (Cambridge, MA: Harvard University Press, 1996).

6. Julia Shaw, *The Memory Illusion: Remembering, Forgetting, and the Science of False Memory*, Kindle e-book (N.p.: Random House Books, 2016).

7. Dan Kapr, *Politely Rejecting the Bible: Why You Shouldn't Believe Everything the Bible Tells You* (Pittsburgh, PA: Enersin Press, 2021).

8. Dale C. Allison, *Jesus of Nazareth: Millenarian Prophet* (Minneapolis, MN: Fortress Press, 1998), 26n69.

9. Craig S. Keener, *Miracles: The Credibility of the New Testament Accounts*, vols. 1 and 2 (Grand Rapids, MI: Baker Academic, 2011). There are important methodological problems with how Keener and other Christian scholars approach these kinds of issues, but that will have to be a discussion for another time.

The Resurrection

1. Dale C. Allison, Jr., *The Resurrection of Jesus: Apologetics, Polemics, History* (New York: Bloomsbury, 2021), 37–44.

2. N. T. Wright, *Surprised by Hope: Rethinking Heaven, the Resurrection, and the Mission of the Church* (New York: HarperOne, 2018), 58–59.

3. Marcus J. Borg, "The Truth of Easter," in Marcus J. Borg and N. T. Wright, *The Meaning of Jesus: Two Views* (New York: HarperOne, 1999), 129.

4. Marcus J. Borg, "The Second Coming Then and Now," in Marcus J. Borg and N. T. Wright, *The Meaning of Jesus: Two Views* (New York: HarperOne, 1999), 195.

5. William Lane Craig, quoted in Lee Strobel, *The Case for Christ: A Journalist's Personal Investigation of the Evidence for Jesus* (Grand Rapids, MI: Zondervan, 1998), 217.

6. See Bart D. Ehrman, *Forgery and Counterforgery: The Use of Literary Deceit in Early Christian Polemics* (Oxford: Oxford University Press, 2013), 171–90, 192–211.

7. For more information about ancient Jewish burial practices, see Craig A. Evans, *Jesus and His World: The Archaeological Evidence* (Louisville, KY: Westminster John Knox Press, 2013), 113–40.

8. C. Behan McCullagh, *Justifying Historical Descriptions* (Cambridge: Cambridge University Press, 1984), 19.

9. Gary R. Habermas and Michael R. Licona, *The Case for the Resurrection of Jesus* (Grand Rapids, MI: Kregel Publications, 2004), 120–21.

10. William Lane Craig, *Reasonable Faith: Christian Truth and Apologetics*, 3rd ed. (Wheaton, IL: Crossway, 2008), 379.

11. Ibid., 382–83.

12. Habermas and Licona, *The Case for the Resurrection of Jesus*, 106–07.

13. Katherine Arcement, "Our Lady of Fatima: The Virgin Mary promised three kids a miracle that 70,000 gathered to see," *The Washington Post*, October 13, 2017, https://www.washingtonpost.com/news/retropolis/wp/2017/10/13/our-lady-of -fatima-the-virgin-mary-promised-three-kids-a-miracle-that-70000-gathered-to-see.

14. Allison, *The Resurrection of Jesus*, 217–21.

15. Wright, *Surprised by Hope*, 58–59.

16. Craig, *Reasonable Faith*, 382–84.

17. Ibid., 109–12.

18. Arthur Conan Doyle, "The Five Orange Pips," in *The Original Illustrated Sherlock Holmes* (New York: Castle Books, n.d.), 69.

Selected Bibliography

Resources for Studying the New Testament

Brown, Raymond E. *An Introduction to the New Testament.* New Haven, CT: Yale University Press, 1997.

Burkett, Delbert. *An Introduction to the New Testament and the Origins of Christianity.* 2nd ed. Cambridge, UK: Cambridge University Press, 2019.

Coogan, Michael D. et al., eds. *The New Oxford Annotated Bible: New Revised Standard Version with the Apocrypha.* 5th ed. Oxford, UK: Oxford University Press, 2018.

Ehrman, Bart D. *The New Testament: A Historical Introduction to the Early Christian Writings.* 7th ed. New York: Oxford University Press, 2020.

Freedman, David Noel, ed. *Eerdmans Dictionary of the Bible.* Grand Rapids, MI: William B. Eerdmans Publishing Company, 2000.

Martin, Dale B. *New Testament History and Literature.* New Haven, CT: Yale University Press, 2012.

Perkins, Pheme. *Reading the New Testament: An Introduction.* 3rd ed. New York: Paulist Press, 2012.

Powell, Mark Allan. *Fortress Introduction to the Gospels.* 2nd ed. Minneapolis, MN: Fortress Press, 2019.

Society of Biblical Literature. *The SBL Study Bible: New Revised Standard Version Updated Edition with the Apocryphal/Deuterocanonical Books.* New York: HarperOne, 2023.

Other Highly Recommended Resources

Allison, Dale C., Jr. *Constructing Jesus: Memory, Imagination, and History.* Grand Rapids, MI: Baker Academic, 2010.

Allison, Dale C., Jr. *The Resurrection of Jesus: Apologetics, Polemics, History.* New York: Bloomsbury, 2021.

Ehrman, Bart D. *Jesus: Apocalyptic Prophet of the New Millennium.* Oxford: Oxford University Press, 1999.

Sanders, E. P. *The Historical Figure of Jesus.* London: Penguin Books, 1995.